AF396506

The Fault Lines of Inequality

Huw Macartney · Johnna Montgomerie ·
Daniela Tepe

The Fault Lines of Inequality

COVID 19 and the Politics of Financialization

palgrave
macmillan

Huw Macartney
University of Birmingham
Birmingham, UK

Johnna Montgomerie
King's College London
London, UK

Daniela Tepe
University of Liverpool
Liverpool, UK

ISBN 978-3-030-96913-4   ISBN 978-3-030-96914-1   (eBook)
https://doi.org/10.1007/978-3-030-96914-1

This Palgrave Macmillan imprint is published by the registered company Springer Nature Switzerland AG
The registered company address is: Gewerbestrasse 11, 6330 Cham, Switzerland

To Sam, Eli, Athena and Helena, Philipp, Robert, Alfred, Marlene and Moritz, Asia, Levi, and Erica.

CONTENTS

List of Figures

CHAPTER 1

An Introduction to Crisis Response

Abstract This chapter introduces the argument that inequality in the UK worsened as a result of the economic policy response to the Covid-19 crisis. We argue that the fault lines of inequality have been driven further apart during the last two years. What we mean by *fault lines* is the social fracturing between stratifications in society, which maps onto income and wealth inequalities. We argue that the economic policy response was a 'routine application' of privatised Keynesianism, an unacknowledged credit-asset policy regime. This led to windfall gains for the top of society while simultaneously taking resources away from the bottom of the distribution who relied on means-tested and time-limited welfare support. We focus on the public policy agenda and make a deliberate challenge to economic policymakers who believe that inequality is the product of individual choices, behavioural preferences, and social capital.

Keywords Inequality · Asset economy · Covid-19 · Fault lines · Economic policy

H. Macartney et al., *The Fault Lines of Inequality*, https://doi.org/10.1007/978-3-030-96914-1_1

1.1   Introduction

As the outbreak of the Covid Pandemic hit its global phase in early 2020, Madonna posted a message on Instagram and Twitter from a bathtub filled with pink rose petals, proclaiming to the world that Covid-19 was the great equaliser: 'we are all in the same boat… and if the ship goes down, we are all going down together […]what is wonderful about it is that it's made us all equal in many ways' (CNN 2020). It was not just Madonna, New York Governor Andrew Cuomo also tweeted in March 2020 this virus was the 'great equaliser' (*Washington Post* 2020a), clearly conflating the universal human condition of having a body with the structural economic conditions those bodies exist in.

Politically, the idea was simple enough—we are all in this together, because it 'affects everyone, rich and poor, black-and-white, urban and rural' (*Washington Post* 2020b). However, rather quickly a starker reality has become visible, despite the delusions of celebrities. In fact, the public did pick up on this reality fairly quickly. Turning to the United Kingdom (UK), the re-elected Conservative government moved away from the initial 'we are all in this together' slogan relatively early on to more differentiating narratives. As it transpires, during the early months of the pandemic Prime Minister Boris Johnson, and his staff in Downing Street were routinely breaking the very rules they were creating and communicating to the nation, indicating that they did never really thought 'we are all in this together'.

As the Covid-19 pandemic rolls on, a shared understanding has emerged, which recognises that we are all in the same storm, yet some of us are aboard small vessels—more likely to capsize—while others are (literally and metaphorically) aboard big and secure cruise liners. And indeed, it always seemed somewhat ironic that a member of the mega-rich global elite saw the 'equalising effect' of the pandemic, at a time when social divides seemed to play such a role in the diverse and unequal experiences of Covid-19.

Picking up the 'different boats' metaphor to stand for inequality between groups in society, this book explores the ways Covid-19 has exacerbated the divisions between the 'haves' and the 'have-nots' in the UK. An established trend of widening economic and social inequality was already visible since 2008 resulting from a decade of austerity. When you dissect the numbers, it is indeed clear that when the pandemic hit, inequality was already bad. Mounting evidence illustrates that experiences of the pandemic varied dramatically. Death rates in deprived communities are significantly higher than among the rich (RSA 2020). Headline figures show the connection between economic deprivation and ill health: people living in the poorest 10% of areas were almost four times more likely to die from Covid-19 than those living in the wealthiest areas (The Health Foundation 2021). Since deprivation clusters in urban areas, the UK's many metropolitan areas were the worst hit in health and economic terms.

It became increasingly clear that established social stratifications can transmit the misfortune of the pandemic along established axes of inequality. For example, in the UK there is an observable racial dimension to Covid-19 inequality, with ethnic minorities tending to live in more deprived, densely populated areas having higher infection rates (Haque et al. 2021). A clear gender dimension can also be seen; women's experiences of the pandemic, in general, have been worse than men's in economic terms, but not in Covid death rates and physical health terms (Women's Budget Group 2020). This is because, while men suffer more physical ill health from the Coronavirus, overall; care responsibilities fall disproportionately on women. This points to the important ways in which public health reflects the political and economic conditions that shape everyday life (Jung et al. 2021). It is telling that a contagious pathogen can easily navigate the social stratifications within society and, by doing so, reflect to us the conditions of human society.

1.2   Covid Fault Lines

Our starting point is the established fault lines of inequality that already existed when the pandemic hit. What we mean by *fault lines* in the context of this book is the social fracturing between stratifications in society, which maps onto income and wealth inequalities but does not determine them. In the UK, the empirical evidence of the fracturing between social groups along the trenches of income and wealth is obvious. Covid is another cause to drive these *fault lines* further apart; it acts like a severe tremor widening the already existing gap in the ice shield. To show how Covid widened the gap, we examine the UK's Covid-19 economic response package, starting from the first national lockdown in March 2020 until January 2022 Underlying this is our belief that how governments responded to a potentially deadly virus threatening human populations across the globe has had an impact. Different responses by governments to curb the spread of the virus produced different outcomes. Here, Covid-19 is the agent of misfortune—it is the cause of the global health crisis and subsequent economic crisis. How governments respond to this shock demonstrates their capacity to mitigate, ameliorate, or deteriorate the conditions under which their citizens live.

Our focus is exclusively on the package of economic measures undertaken, not the public health measures. While we acknowledge that public health and economic health are intertwined, we focus on the economic policy response and its connection to outcomes in everyday life. This outlook differs from interpretations of the pandemic response that focus on elite politics and the unprecedented scale of coordination and apparent nature of intervention seen and required to address a global pandemic. For such interpretations, the UK's governmental intervention was hailed as a complete change of direction due to apparent unprecedented scale of public spending after years of commitment to fiscal austerity (*The Economist* 2021). The 2021 Budget was reported as a turning point for British Conservatism, recognising the role the state plays in the economy and society and drawing parallels to Keynesian tax and spend of the 1950s (Parker et al. 2021). In contrast to the theme of unprecedented event and response, our emphasis focuses on the substantial continuity we can identify.

Put simply, the economic policy response was a routine application of 'Privatised Keynesianism' as a crisis response yet with some time limited emergency measures added to the mix. Colin Crouch (2009) initially articulated this 'unacknowledged' credit-asset policy regime in the UK—as the 2008 global financial crisis showed—which we can identify in the current crisis response.

Since the 2008 global financial crisis, the consensus of the UK economic public policy agenda is to rely on expansionary monetary policy and minimal fiscal policy, which entrench established income and wealth stratifications, as the main levers of distribution. Covid-19 activated a similar economic crisis response, shown in these two representative figures: on the one hand, the Treasury's (2020) summary of emergency fiscal measures at £250 billion in the fiscal year 2020–21 (£105 for public services, £82 billion to support households, £62 billion for business), compared to the Bank of England's (2020) £895 billion in the half-year March 2020 to November 2020, stand in stark contrast.

By the 2021 Autumn statement, the UK Treasury strategy is to commit to an additional £150 billion in departmental funding, £177 billion for health care, £4.7 billion for education, and a litany of other small-scale pockets (Rishi Sunak MP 2021). However, this spending is nowhere near the amount the Treasury underwrites when the Bank of England extends its balance sheet further with little democratic oversight. As with any national emergency, there was little time as Covid-19 unfolded to deliberate about the most appropriate policy mix. It is clear the same state resource allocation template was and still is applied that has been in use before, expanding the central bank's balance sheet and constrain the expansion of fiscal commitments. These policies reproduce existing asset-based inequalities, rather than mitigate the effects of the economic shock. Therefore, we argue that if you are looking for someone to blame for rising inequality, look no further than UK state managers. Decisions and indecisions taken during 2020–2021 compounded the devastating dynamics of the asset economy on economic inequality.

Against this background, we argue that you cannot understand why inequality is getting wider because of Covid-19 unless you understand how government support for asset-based economic policy from the central bank, combined with decreasing funding for social security from the Treasury, reproduces and widens inequality in the first place. Politically, governments make choices that are informed by narratives and ideologies, which in turn create policies that govern society. In the UK, it is readily observed that governments justify their choices to routinely bailout financial markets by reference to how crucial it is for systemic stability, thus (purportedly) benefiting everyone. Continued support for the asset economy to expand without limit, while rolling back social welfare in the name of fiscal prudence, jettisons large segments of society to be responsible for their own (mis)fortune. This is the reason why Covid-19 exacerbated inequality. Post-war nostalgia aside, the UK's Covid-19 economic response, from March 2020 to the 2021 Budget is entirely consistent with privatised Keynesianism. Further, we contend the current trend of worsening wealth inequality will continue because of the reliance on the credit-driven asset economy and temporary means-tested welfare provision.

Thus, this is not simply a book about different experiences of the pandemic in the UK. Nor is it simply a book stating the ongoing existence of inequality. We also do not stop at saying pre-existing inequalities meant that individuals and communities fared differently. This is the equivalent of saying Mrs Jones (a rich woman) had a better experience of the pandemic than Mrs Bloggs (a poor woman) because Mrs Jones had more money going into the pandemic. This is a bland and unremarkable point. Instead, we explain how the pandemic meant that Mrs Jones got richer, or Mrs Bloggs got poorer, meaning that what divides them intensified because of the pandemic, or that what separates the poles in society became wider as a result. Importantly, Mrs Jones and Bloggs did not choose different paths, they encountered the pandemic and found themselves further apart as a result.

This is important because it puts (often unrecognised) responsibility for inequality with the state, in the resource allocation choices made in economic policies rather than choices made by the individual. This is an important focus of analysis of Covid-19—which was undoubtedly an unexpected event. The state governs society, whether politicians in government or civil servants in departments; they make decisions about how to allocate state resources. In other words, we look at policymaking during the pandemic, especially in the Treasury and central bank, because it has profound impacts on levels of inequality in society.

Thus, if we stipulate that inequality is the product of established political decisions which disproportionately benefited some segments of society, then this is an important conclusion with controversial political implications. On the one hand, the immediate UK pandemic response has seen many emergency measures implemented, for instance furlough packages were widely distributed, and the economic bounce-back is gathering pace. This might lead some to conclude that successful measures prevented inequality from getting worse. Yet, when we look at the national economic indicators early on the picture is mixed, but not ambiguous or unclear. For instance, job losses and the lack of a furlough safety net in many cases sank heavily indebted households even further into a financial black hole; while the rich and some middle-income households saved on travel and consumption costs and saw their savings and investments increase (House of Commons 2021b: 11).

On the other hand, the way the UK's pandemic response is moving in its later stages creates the same 'unfortunate' distributional outcomes as with the 2007–2008 financial crisis. For instance, the so-called unconventional monetary policy benefits only the wealthiest asset holders. Meanwhile temporary emergency measures, like furlough and the Universal Credit uplift, are withdrawn for middle and lower strata of society. To put it bluntly, the idea that government policy decisions benefited some more than others implies that either—in the worst-case scenario—policymakers believe certain individuals and households are more worthy of state resources than others; or—in the best-case scenario—that state managers subscribed to an economic model which caused severe social and economic harm unconsciously. If either of these scenarios is true, it is extremely alarming that inequality is worsening, contributing to the failure to address the long-term political and social crisis facing the UK (Macartney 2019; Montgomerie and Tepe-Belfrage 2020).

The purpose of the book is to unpack these very questions of decisions and choices. Not those made by any individual—rather, specifically focusing on public policy as indicative of the resource allocation decisions of the state. First, via asset-based welfare which promotes integration of individuals into global financial markets through ownership of an investment portfolio and residential housing. Second, via means-tested welfare, which promotes individualised responsibility and a limited social security net. These two public policy prongs generate overlapping forms of economic inequality. Focusing on the public policy agenda and inequality is a deliberate challenge to economic policymakers who believe that inequality is the product of individual choices, behavioural preferences, and social capital. This book looks at the structural causes of inequality and its links to the privatised Keynesian policy agenda. Our view is that the asset economy acts as a driving force of inequality.

1.3   Outline of Book

To substantiate this argument, we use a simple framework to evaluate inequality as a hierarchy of the top, middle, and bottom strata of the UK economy and society. There is little doubt that income and wealth inequality in the UK exists (Atkinson 2015; Lansley 2012; Savage 2021). Still, it is contentious to suggest the gulf between these groups is widening. To show this, we look at the choices of government on how to generate and distribute its resources across society. We inflect this analysis with a full recognition that social stratification intersects with economic inequality and that comparable stories about worsening inequality could be told with a greater focus on the racial and gendered dynamics of the pandemic. Yet, we choose to view the inequality question through the lens of economic inequality—primarily for analytical purposes—which make clear the choices of policymakers in this area.

Chapter 2 provides the context, the big picture account of the connection between the rise of the asset economy and widening inequality over the past two decades, in income and wealth terms. Space limits a more substantive engagement with the rich literature on income and wealth inequality in the UK. Starting with Thomas Piketty's (Piketty 2014; also see: Boushey et al. 2017) intervention into understanding of economic inequality as the distribution between earned and unearned income; including established understandings of Anglo-American Privatised Keynesianism asset-based welfare as a policy paradigm; and ending up at Adkins, Cooper, and Koning's (Adkins et al. 2020, 2021) evaluation and framework of the Asset Economy. We provide a basic outline of inequality in the UK before Covid-19 strikes; these are the established fault lines between the top, middle, and bottom strata of society. We examine the UK Covid-19 economic response in the context of these existing stratifications.

Chapter 3 examines those at the top of the distribution in income and wealth terms and explains how Covid-19 response measures made them wealthier. Crisis responses here include the cutting of interest rates for corporate borrowers and (un)conventional monetary policy to open credit-flow by extending reserves and using credit-subsidies (Bank of England 2021). In the first three months of the Covid response alone, £895 billion were injected, providing ample bank reserves to lend which directly benefited asset markets with corporate bond purchases (Bank of England 2020). To stabilise financial markets the Bank of England once again drove up asset prices—which are heavily concentrated in the hands of the rich. A Resolution Foundation report (Leslie and Shah 2021) analysed existing UK data sources to show that the combined effects of asset-price appreciation contributed £756 billion of the total wealth (£890 billion) increased during the pandemic. Most of these result from changes in asset prices which have led to this increase. 'The richest households have seen the largest wealth increases in absolute terms, reflecting their larger existing wealth holdings on entering the crisis' (p. 31). Asset inequality is the fault line in which those who benefit from economic crisis 'response measures' are not those that earn wages and incomes, but those that own assets—this force is driving the gulf between social strata even further apart.

Chapter 4 provides a picture of the middle, or 60% of the UK population, what is often considered the majority of households that rely heavily on earned income and has small asset-holdings. Covid-19 response measures sought to put a floor, to protect the middle from experiencing free-fall. The Job Retention Scheme (CJRS, called furlough) provided direct income subsidies to those that qualified—salaried (pay-as-you-earn) employees earning up to £2,500 per month—to prevent income shocks in the middle. The latest HMRC figures show the value of cumulative claims through furlough at £57.7 billion reaching a peak of 2.7 million claims in August 2020—up from 1.2 million in May 2020 (HMRC 2020). Monetary policy provided credit and the Treasury stamp duty tax-relief helped to stimulate house-price inflation, giving homeowners an uplift in their perceived residential housing values. Similarly, stock market gains kept portfolio investments profitable and the middle less fearful. However, overall gains are patchy as many in the middle are also small-business owners, consultants, and undertake other forms of well-paid contractual work, which did not have access to any government support.

Chapter 5 details how those at the bottom, in income and wealth terms, fared in the Covid-19 response especially given the substantial fiscal response. Recent ONS analysis clearly shows those in the lowest income deciles on the distribution, those who were working (43.8%) or unemployed (30.4%), were more likely to report reduced household income between April and October 2020 (ONS 2020). Yet, beyond income losses, there is the harsh reality facing those on low incomes after years of austerity. The UK welfare state has provided a threadbare safety net to those at the bottom, there are large gaps in coverage and only minimal support for those who do qualify. Football player Marcus Rashford's campaign and policy victory brought the issue of free school meals during school holidays for underprivileged children to light. Here, we can see a flash point between public morality and the Dickensian morality of the Treasury. Yet, again, while Covid-19 has helped to shed a light on the issue, food poverty is not a new problem. A record 2.5 million food parcels were distributed between April 2020 and March 2021 by the Trussell Trust (Trussell Trust 2021) and almost 2 million children went hungry in the UK in 2020 (Wales Online 2020). The number of food parcels distributed only highlights the tip of the iceberg when it comes to child suffering. In 2019–20, 4.3 million children—or 31% of the child population—were classified as living in poverty (CPAG 2021). Indeed, research published by the TUC in July 2021 revealed that more than a million children from (keyworker) households in the front line of the fight against the coronavirus pandemic were living in poverty (*The Guardian* 2021). This chapter shows how holes in the safety net have further deteriorated, rather than ameliorated, due to the pandemic response.

Finally, we conclude with considerations for policymakers, and those being governed, about what the return to normal really means in the UK and how we would like to see the new normal look different. Inequality matters, making this case is the motivation for writing this book. Covid-19 has highlighted that inequality remains a fundamental challenge requiring greater attention in research, policy, and with the public. Like Covid-19, inequality is not going away. Due to a persistent reliance on the privatised Keynesian asset economy, there is limited scope for the so-called 'levelling up' agenda to work. Importantly, we believe another future is possible. We dream of a better society, caring, ecologically sustainable, equal, and prosperous.

1.4   Plea to Policymakers
for a Progressive Public Policy

Inequality must be addressed through public policy, as we are not holding out hope for a revolution. This book tries to make the case for making the reduction of inequality a key feature of the current pandemic recovery paradigm. We align with the growing number of progressive economists and policymakers calling for green care-led recovery capable of reversing inequality trends and able to create a stable as well as a sustainable economy (Blundell et al. 2020; De Henau and Himmelweit 2020; Women's Budget Group 2021). Misfortune and suffering have become a defining feature of the unequal distribution of (in)humanity during the pandemic. If we are indeed to accept that a revolution to end all inequality is impossible in our lifetimes, then it is our duty to find ways to use policy to mitigate against climate and human crises. At the very least making the lives of those suffering most from an unequal economy better, while working towards a just and prosperous society.

That inequality matters is undeniable. In the UK economic inequality is arguably among the 'greatest social threat[s] of our times' (Dorling 2014: 14). Also, the wider public has caught up with more academic concerns about inequality. The British Social Attitudes Survey—for example—has repeatedly shown growing public resentment towards the causes and effects of inequality: in 2017 the survey found that more people (42%) agreed than disagreed (28%) with the idea that government should redistribute income from the better-off to those who are less well-off. By 2019, the Survey found that 65% of participants believed there was 'quite a lot' of poverty in Britain, and this view too had increased by 13% since 2006

(2019: 2). Inequality breeds division in society. We would go as far as to say that some of the most high-profile political developments in the UK over the last decade and a half are entangled with inequality. From Occupy St Paul's to Brexit, to Black Lives Matter, and anti-lockdown protest movements—the tensions caused by the fault lines of inequality erupt at different pressure points. Economic inequality creates bigger social problems than merely division, evidenced by the UK transforming into one of the most deprived societies in the western world.

Covid-19 teaches a necessary lesson about income and wealth inequality—it has life and death implications for people. The UK death rates from Covid-19 are among the worst among the industrialised world, the most unequal were the worst affected. Policymakers were committed to mitigating the negative impact on the economy of public health measures. This is not a new story, connections between public policy and deprivation are well told by epidemiologists Pickett and Wilkinson (2010) in *The Spirit Level*, which details across a large cross-section of countries how domestic economic inequality is the cause of many social ills in wealthy societies. For some time, there is a growing acceptance of the importance of well-being over economic growth among scholars (Durand 2015; O'Hara 2014; Stiglitz et al. 2010), and this needs to again be prioritised over asset-inflation and interest rates. Economic wealth provides tangible security and well-being—specifically, the absence of it causes suffering and untimely death.

The Covid-19 pandemic response exposed how government policymaking can have positive or traumatic social outcomes. The state is not a passive bystander and economic policy is not simply technocratic. We use public policy as a way of understanding how the state transforms the organisation of the economy and society. Our understanding of the asset economy traces it to the liberalisation of financial markets from the 1980s when wealth inequality began to worsen—these policy measures disproportionately benefited asset owners. First, through private pension schemes that were actively encouraged via tax incentives and at the same time state subsidised. Also, homeownership became a central feature of how the asset economy radiates out into everyday life. At the national level an 'unacknowledged' policy regime 'Privatised Keynesianism' relied on credit-fuelled asset growth to drive wealth and debt-driven consumption to maintain effective demand (Gamble 2014; Hay 2013; Montgomerie and Tepe-Belfrage 2017). The social safety net—welfare and social spending—was replaced by increased means-testing and minimalist support. Now, individuals were 'responsible' for their own fortune, and misfortune. Those in society that relied on the state to provide income support or social security saw welfare provision steadily withdrawn (see House of Commons 2021: 38).

In sum, there was already a growing sense of public backlash against inequality, after a decade of austerity; the cruel misfortune brought by the pandemic will—almost certainly—heighten these tensions. These winds push at a need for greater willingness to consider a progressive economic blueprint. The asset economy creates runaway wealth at the top and has also benefited the critical 'middle' mass of homeowners (through house-price rises) in society. However, stagnating incomes, growing inflation, and a means-tested welfare state creates the 'squeezed middle', which increases appetite for change. In a sense, this is the dilemma at the heart of the asset economy, because the largest proportion (60+%) of the British public fall into this category where the asset economy can be an agent of fortune or misfortune, depending on how the wheel turns. For those unable to fully participate in the asset economy, a precarious existence is legitimised by austere public policy and a discourse that demonises poverty as individual failure.

References

Adkins, L., M. Cooper, and M. Konings. 2020. *The asset economy*. Wiley.

Adkins, L., M. Cooper, and M. Konings. 2021. Class in the 21st century: Asset inflation and the new logic of inequality. *Environment and Planning a: Economy and Space* 53 (3): 548–572.

Atkinson, A.B. 2015. *Inequality: What can be done?* Harvard University Press.

Bank of England. 2020. Quantitative easing—Fact sheet, gov.co.uk, November. Available at: https://www.bankofengland.co.uk/monetary-policy/quantitative-easing. Accessed 12 November 2021.

Bank of England. 2021. Our response to coronavirus (Covid), 21 January. Available at: https://www.bankofengland.co.uk/coronavirus. Accessed 22 April 2021.

Blundell, R., R. Joyce, M.C. Dias, and X. Xu. 2020. *Covid-19: The impacts of the pandemic on inequality* [Briefing note]. Institute for Fiscal Studies (IFS).

Boushey, H., J.B. DeLong, and M. Steinbaum. 2017. *After Piketty: The agenda for economics and inequality*. Harvard University Press.

CNN. 2020. Coronavirus is the great equaliser, Madonna tells fans from her bathtub, 23 March.

CPAG. 2021. *Child Poverty Facts and Figures*. Child Poverty Action Group.

Crouch, C. 2009. Privatised Keynesianism: An unacknowledged policy regime. *BJPIR* 11: 382–399.

Dorling, D. 2014. *Inequality and the 1%*, 2nd ed. London and New York: Verso Books.

Dorling, D. 2019. *Inequality and the 1%*, 2nd ed. London and New York: Verso Books.

Durand, M. 2015. The OECD better life initiative: How's life? And the measurement of well-being. *Review of Income and Wealth* 61 (1): 4–17.

Gamble, A. 2014. *Crisis without end?: The unravelling of Western prosperity*. Palgrave Macmillan.

Haque, Z., L. Becares, and N. Treloar. 2021. *Over-exposed and under-protected* (p. 24) [Research Report]. Runnymede Trust.

Hay, C. 2013. *The failure of Anglo-Liberal capitalism*. Palgrave Macmillan.

Henau, J. D., and S. Himmelweit. 2020. *A Care-led Recovery from Coronavirus*. Women's Budget Group.

HMRC. 2020. HMRC coronavirus (COVID-19) statistics, gov.co.uk, 12 May. Available at: https://www.gov.uk/government/collections/hmrc-cor onavirus-covid-19-statistics. Accessed 12 November 2021.

House of Commons. 2021a. *Coronavirus: Universal Credit during the Crisis*. House of Commons Briefing Paper No. 8999, 15 January.

House of Commons. 2021b. *Coronavirus: Impact on household savings and debt*. House of Commons Briefing Paper No. 9060.

Jung, J., J. Manley, and V. Shrestha. 2021. Coronavirus infections and deaths by poverty status: The effects of social distancing. *Journal of Economic Behavior & Organization* 182: 311–330.

Lansley, S. 2012. *The cost of inequality: Why equality is essential for recovery*. Gibson Square.

Leslie, J., and K. Shah. 2021. The Wealth Gap Year: The impact of the coronavirus crisis on UK household wealth. The Resolution Foundation. Available at: https://www.resolutionfoundation.org/app/uploads/2021/07/Wea lth-gap-year.pdf.

Macartney, H. 2019. *The bank culture debate: Ethics, values and financialisation in Anglo-America*. Oxford University Press.

Montgomerie, J., and D. Tepe-Belfrage. 2017. Caring for debts: How the household economy exposes the limits of financialisation. *Critical Sociology* 43 (4–5): 653–668.

Montgomerie, J., and D. Tepe-Belfrage. 2020. Financialisation, crisis and austerity as the distribution of harm. In *The Routledge Handbook of Critical European Studies*. Routledge.

O'Hara, S. 2014. Everything needs care: Towards a context-based economy. In *Counting on Marilyn Waring: New Advances in Feminist Economics*, ed. M. Bjørnholt and A. McKay. Demeter Press.

ONS. 2020. Personal and economic well-being in Great Britain. Office for National Statistics. Available at: https://www.ons.gov.uk/peoplepopulationandcommunity/wellbeing/bulletins/personalandeconomicwellbeingintheuk/january2021#savings-borrowing-and-affordability. Accessed 12 November 2021.

Parker, G., D. Strauss, and T. Stubbington. 2021. Budget 2021: Rishi Sunak sets out 'moral' mission to limit state and cut taxes. *Financial Times*, 27 October. Available at: https://www.ft.com/content/e7c84fbe-0857-4de8-85c1-ed81f870a4f5. Accessed 12 November 2021.

Pickett, K., and R. Wilkinson. 2010. *The Spirit Level: Why Equality Is Better for Everyone*. Penguin UK.

Piketty, T. 2014. *Capital in the Twenty-First Century*, trans. A. Goldhammer. Cambridge, MA: Harvard University Press.

Rishi Sunak MP. 2021. Budget Speech 2021. Autumn Statementpresented at the Budget, House of Commons, UK Parliament, 27 October. Available at: https://www.gov.uk/government/speeches/budget-speech-2021. Accessed 12 November 2021.

RSA. 2020. COVID-19 vaccine deployment: Behaviour, ethics, misinformation and policy strategies. *Royal Society*, 21 October.

Savage, M. 2021. *The return of inequality: Social change and the weight of the past*. Harvard University Press.

Stiglitz, J.E., A. Sen, and J.-P. Fitoussi. 2010. *Mismeasuring our lives: Why GDP doesn't add up*. New York: The New Press.

The Economist. 2021. Boris Johnson's Conservatives plan to create a bigger, busier state, 11 March. Available at: https://www.economist.com/britain/2021/11/06/boris-johnsons-conservatives-plan-to-create-a-bigger-busier-state. Accessed 12 November 2021.

The Guardian. 2021. Number of billionaires in UK reached new record during Covid crisis, 21 May.

The Health Foundation. 2021. *Unequal Pandemic, fairer recovery: The covid-19 impact inquiry report, July 2021*. London: The Health Foundation.

Trussell Trust. 2021. More than 5,100 food parcels given to people facing crisis across the UK every day in past six months, says the Trussell Trust, 24 November.

Wales Online. 2020. Almost two million children went hungry in the UK in 2020, 9 December.

Washington Post. 2020a. Gov. Cuomo is wrong, covid-19 is anything but a great equalizer, 5th April.

Washington Post. 2020b. The pandemic is dramatically deepening inequality, 15 October.

Women's Budget Group. 2020. Submission to the Women and Equalities Select Committee inquiry: Unequal impact? Coronavirus and the gendered economic impact, June. Available at: https://wbg.org.uk/wp-content/upl oads/2020/06/WBG-Gender-economic-impact-submission.pdf. Accessed 9 April 2021.

Women's Budget Group. 2021. Social Care, Gender and Covid-19. Available at: https://wbg.org.uk/wp-content/uploads/2021/03/Social-care-gen der-and-Covid-19.pdf. Accessed 26 April 2021.

CHAPTER 2

Inequality and the Asset Economy

Abstract This chapter develops the analytical framework for the remainder of the book by examining the fault lines of inequality in the UK. We argue that robust support for the asset economy reinforced existing structures of wealth creation via asset markets which were distributed unevenly across society long before the pandemic hit. Asset ownership and the types of debt influenced the degree and types of state support provided. These are fault lines of inequality in the UK that divide the top, the middle, and the bottom of society. The economic policy response to COVID-19 made inequality worse as government intervention put a floor under asset-market losses while providing insufficient support to the asset poor to make up for losses experienced as a result of the crisis. Divisions in society thus have deepened despite the unprecedented amount of money allocated to support the UK economy during the pandemic.

Keywords Asset economy · Privatised Keynesianism · Inequality · Welfare retreat

H. Macartney et al., *The Fault Lines of Inequality*,
https://doi.org/10.1007/978-3-030-96914-1_2

2.1   INTRODUCTION

President Barack Obama called inequality 'the defining challenge of our time' because its effects are widespread and impact society deeply (as quoted in Bump 2013). This statement stands in stark contrast to long-held economic assumptions of politicians that inequality would automatically reduce over time and thus could be left unaddressed. Further, claiming inequality exists as a political problem, let alone that it is the defining feature of our time, challenges the established view among economists, that as markets develop, they evolve almost inevitably towards more egalitarian societies (further to: Kuznets 1955; Solow 1974). And indeed, development economists held until recently the rather optimistic view that automatic income and wealth equalisers would distribute the gains made by increased productivity not just throughout but *evenly* throughout society (Syll 2014: 36).

In the specific area of economic inequality, governments tend to rely on the normative public policy frame of providing equality of 'opportunity' not equality of 'outcome'. When this common narrative is applied in public policy it frames inequality as a 'ladder' or 'staircase' in which each step represents an income or wealth quartile (25% grouping of income or wealth holders). Those that are socially mobile climb up each step (or rung of the ladder) by earning more income or acquiring more wealth. It is the individual who makes choices, acquires skills, and enacts the movement upward and downward. With this understanding of inequality, policymakers can design ways to 'nudge' or influence behavioural association and patterns that give people skills to move upward on the income and wealth ladder. Also, states can invest in capabilities or well-being, to improve an individual's opportunity to move upward. Among other things, this leads to an emphasis on the relationship between technology and education; the idea that growth in skill-biased technologies has allegedly increased the desirability of the highly educated group, making them more marketable and raising their wages (Syll 2014: 37). Wages reflect your contribution to economic output in this model. So, if you are poor, it is your own fault, a product of your own ineptitude, or failure as an individual.

Yet, inequality is worsening in the wealthiest, so-called advanced Western capitalist economies, with the UK ahead of the curve because of its dependence on an asset economy (see most recently: Adkins et al. 2021; Christophers 2020; Savage 2021). By 2014, the UK had already reached the stage where the richest top tenth of adults over 20 were taking four times the average income, while the remaining 90% were surviving on 0.67% of the average income (Dorling 2019: ix). Another measure puts the top 1% of UK individuals' take-home income at approximately 8% of the entire amount of income earned by all individuals (IFS 2020) and 42% of all disposable household income went to the 20% of people with the highest household incomes (UK Parliament 2020). Meanwhile the top 1% took a multiple of fifteen times the average income, while the top 0.1% recorded a massive 67 times the average (Dorling 2019). These figures are indicative of not just economic trends, but as Pickett and Wilkinson (2010; see also: Pickett 2019) demonstrated through epidemiological extensive analysis—economic inequality can perpetuate many societal ills. This is especially true within the wealthiest countries, and in the UK. These figures do not adhere to the equality of opportunity view, these are systemic inequalities—meaning it is not just the individuals' failure to succeed, there is a clear failure of state and market relations to provide that opportunity.

2.2 THE ASCENT OF FINANCE AND THE POLITICS OF FINANCIALISATION

What is missed in this economic framing of inequality is the transformation of the UK economy since the 1980s that produces inequality of opportunity and outcome. A more pragmatic and historical perspective on inequality in the UK recognises it has gone hand-in-hand with the financialisation of the economy (from, Froud et al. 2001; to, Christophers 2020). The growing significance of financial services to the overall UK economy reflected a shift in economic thinking. In the post-war period, especially in the Anglo-American countries, the public policy paradigm recognised that individual and economic well-being was generated by income from employment in markets and welfare provision from the state, the so-called Keynesian welfare state. Democratic capitalism—the name given to the economic order established in the west after the Second World War—involved an inherently conflictual relationship between capitalist markets and democratic politics (Streeck 2014). For a time, we are told, these conflicting pressures were kept in check. This was achieved by a social democratic compromise between markets and voters. The longevity of this compromise was aided by reasonably consistent levels of economic growth (and robust welfare provision). This economic growth facilitated wage gains. And these wage gains contributed to reduced divisions between the rich and poor, or lower levels of economic inequality.

In other words, as salaries increased and levels of inequality were reduced following the second world war, the critical mass of people were willing to accept the given socioeconomic order (Nunn and Tepe-Belfrage, forthcoming). From the 1980s onwards however, as transnational corporations began changing their corporate structures, a process labelled financialization took hold (Epstein 2005; Lazonick and O'Sullivan 2000). It shifted the production-based model of post-war capitalism, the production and trade of things; to an asset-based model of market growth, based on assets and trade in services. Overall, this shift saw a slowdown in wage growth in traditional jobs. Yet for those working in the financial services and corporate sector, this shift brought income from other sources, namely financial assets. To simplify, the shift away from the production-based economy fuelled the shift away from income from wage labour (Froud et al. 2001). A new and dynamic public policy paradigm emerged to support financialisation, applying some of the aforementioned insights about markets and individuals (Best 2005; Krippner 2011). Financialisation opened the door for asset ownership as the defining characteristic of many advanced capitalist economies and played an especially important role in the UK.

The politics of financialisaton, in the UK specifically, is best understood as a major shift in the ideas that inform economic policy. Put simply, the biggest change was to move away from full employment and wage growth as engines of GDP, towards fostering an investor-friendly climate; and to abandon universal welfare in trade for asset ownership and means-tested emergency state support from the 1980s. Constructing an investor-friendly climate gave rise to monetary policy focused on price stability and inflation targeting, at the expense of full employment. The 'politics of sound money' was the rallying cry of technocrats echoed by the central bank with the purpose of signalling to investors that asset-based wealth accumulation would be protected against inflation. In the early 2000s, historically low levels of inflation and low-interest rates combined to fuel rising asset prices (Hay 2009, 2011). The politics of inflation-targeting from the 1980s created the technocratic conditions that permitted loose monetary policy in the 2000s. When this built up to the 2008 global financial crisis, UK policymakers turned to repeated rounds of asset-purchase programmes to continue supporting an investor-friendly climate. Policymakers predominantly relied on central-bank interventions to ensure that financial markets continued to grow. This ensured ongoing rising asset prices despite the 2008 financial crisis continuing to benefit asset holders and the rich, while simultaneously increasing levels of inequality in the lead up to the pandemic.

And indeed, the distributional effects of the Anglo finance-led growth model have created an ever-growing divide between the rich and the poor. Tendentially, policymakers tend to focus on the distributional outcomes of fiscal policy at the expense of considering structural conditions in markets as well as monetary policy. In the aftermath of the 2008 financial crisis however, the 'distributional implications of *monetary* policy have received more attention' (Hohberger et al. 2019: 2). This is a non-trivial shift in the debate about inequality because central banks have generally balked at claims that monetary policy had discernible distributional effects, on the grounds that this expanded focus would entail a 'damaging loss of independence and a dangerous distraction from their core competencies' (Honohan 2019: 2). Historically, by focusing primarily on essentially defensive goals of price and financial stability, central banks managed to avoid debates about the impact of monetary policy on different groups in the economy, asserting the effects were neutral.

2.3   The Asset Economy and Asset-Based Welfare

The important historical context of the rise of financialisation in the UK, which involves transformations in both financial markets as well as public policy priorities, is distilled here into a simple frame—*The Asset Economy*—which Lisa Adkins, Malinda Cooper, and Martijn Konings (2020) put forward as both structural, in terms of the primacy of assets over commodities, and intersubjective, in which asset logics embed expectations of wealth gains at higher-rates than wage gains (this chapter and Chapter 3). This framing, as it relates to the UK, explains how several decades of house-price increases turned residential property into a lucrative financial asset, not just for the middle-class but for the so-called 1% as well. It explains how the asset economy creates a 'lock-in' effect where the credit-fuelled asset-price increases become essential, as much for individual sense of well-being as for macroeconomic growth. In turn, they elaborate on this dynamic and how it shapes the contours of inequality: those with income from assets have seen wealth gains go up much more and faster than those that rely on income from employment

(Chapter 4). Adkins et al.'s (2020) contribution elegantly ties together significant insights into why financialisation intensifies inequality: asset markets concentrate wealth in the hands of those that already have it. When the financial market crisis struck, financial bailouts and a decade of monetary policy facilitated further wealth gains for those that already owned assets, widening the gulf with those groups that do not. We focus on housing as Adkins et al. do, as a central pillar of the asset economy, generating wealth gains for the wealthiest in society and acting as a staple of middle-class financial security while excluding—due to unaffordability—ever-larger segments of the population.

This connects directly to a key feature of financialisation, especially in the UK: the degree to which economic policy sought to 'democratize' finance or integrate finance into the everyday life of its citizens. Ideas around asset-based welfare can be traced back to discussions about minimum income guarantees in the early 1990s and the belief that asset gains would be the better alternative. As Watson (2009) highlighted, the assumption—derived from orthodox Economics—was that instrumentally rational individuals would support (consent to) the prevailing structure of society in exchange for some guarantees about access to resources, enabling life to be lived 'in a dignified manner' (43). The emergence of the asset economy was thus essentially a politically driven shift towards 'welfare self-reliance' (Ronald 2008; Schwartz and Seabrooke 2008). Rather than 'relying on social transfers to counter welfare insecurity, individuals themselves were increasingly expected to accept greater personal responsibility for accumulating assets that enabled them to make their own welfare arrangements' (Ronald et al. 2017: 176).

In the UK, the move away from universalism in government-funded welfare provisions began apace in the 1980s/1990s. The asset-based system of welfare was normalised as the socially appropriate means of protecting future consumption in the absence of state provision (Lowe et al. 2012; Toussaint and Elsinga 2009). Indeed, in countries like the UK, governments used *housing markets* 'to pursue non-housing goals in regard to key areas of personal well-being such as health, education and pension provision' (Ronald and Elsinga 2012; Malpass 2008: 3). Put simply, it was assumed that people would adjust to and cope with cuts to government welfare if some alternative, self-initiated means of (economic) survival were established.

Asset-based welfare appeals to economists because it implies a degree of rationality to decisions about the balance between consumption (in the present) and welfare (in the future). It is said to allow individuals to plan for a secure financial future when for example income from labour may be lower but the demand for welfare has increased (in older age for example). This kind of assumed economic rationality underpins and legitimises government decisions placing the burden for welfare on the individual. In other words, governments applied the following message: since money (welfare spending) does not grow on trees you will need to provide for yourself, and private pensions or homeownership (for those who can achieve it) is the method we would recommend. Mapping the political dimensions of financialisation thus, we see an overlap between government policy, the asset economy, and everyday life.

2.4   Perpetual Crisis and Response in the Asset Economy

When the 2008 global financial crisis hit, the UK government coordinated massive bailouts because finance was seen as strategically important. The investor climate mentality of states sought to prioritise stability over reform. Initial emergency fiscal measures became a long-term commitment to successive rounds of Quantitative Easing (QE) by the Bank of England. Initially framed as extraordinary monetary measures, expanding reserves and buying up toxic assets became normalised as credit-enhancements and strategic bonds-buying. As central banks began wide-scale asset-purchase programmes the market price of such assets (bonds) continued upward. Monetary policy intervention is intended to pump large amounts of liquidity into the financial system in the expectation that banks and financial institutions will increase lending leading to greater investment, growth, and higher levels of employment (BoE 2020). Monetary policymakers argue that QE works through the so-called bank lending channel that would assist the economy; but a growing body of criticisms argue that quantitative easing works through a different—asset-price—channel (Brookings 2015).

Independent of how it works, in the UK at least, we can conclude that the economic recovery experienced since the global financial crisis—the period of QE—was also the 'first lost decade [of wages growth] since the 1860s' (Giles 2016). This was primarily because, despite QE, the UK had experienced a 16% shortfall of productivity growth since 2008 compared with the prior trend. There are some studies which argue that QE did have a positive impact on the real economy and economic growth (Beck et al. 2019). As the economy recovers, wages rise, so we are told. So some would argue that—in the long run—everyone will benefit from QE and that rising wealth for rich asset owners is only the immediate, short-term effect of central-bank programmes.

Among those making these arguments is the United States National Bureau of Economic Research (NBER 2020)—here central-bank economists evaluate central-bank policies. And indeed, it is not just us who are sceptical about the degree of independence in these analyses. Others have accused these studies of being partial and biased. Central bank economists appear to have attached an overwhelmingly positive assessment of QE in boosting growth and lifting inflation. For example, 'Martin Weale, a member of the BoE's interest-rate setting Monetary Policy Committee, found asset purchases worth 1% of national income boosted UK gross domestic product by about 0.18% and inflation by 0.3%. [And] a study by John Williams, president of the San Francisco Federal Reserve, concluded that asset purchases had reduced the US unemployment rate by 1.5 percentage points by late 2012 and helped the economy avoid deflation' (*Financial Times* 2015). And yet research by the NBER found that papers published by non-central-bank economists were more sceptical of the impact QE had had. For instance, the NBER paper argued that central-bank findings 'report systematically larger effects of QE on both output and inflation' (WSJ 2020). In other words, positive assessments of QE—and its distributional effects—are highly questionable (NBER 2020).

What is clear is that monetary policy, especially post financial market crisis, is a key mechanism for supporting the asset economy. In the UK, successive rounds of (un)conventional monetary policy for well over a decade have had profound economic and social effects. This means that central banks—contrary to their own claims—have contributed to rising inequality by influencing asset prices. This is an explosive claim because it implies that the market-led process of financialisation is not the only cause of wealth inequality. Instead, it implies that the state has played a vital role; central-bank long-term asset purchases boosted 'prices of financial assets that are disproportionately owned by wealthier households' (Forbes 2015). Much of the focus of the criticism over the past decade has been on the impact of monetary policy on the distribution of wealth. Cross-country survey studies have found that quantitative easing has had no discernible impact on employment and growth that would have helped a wider range of social groups (Williamson 2017;

Macartney 2019). Also, that lower income households did not benefit from these programmes nor from the accompanying rise in asset values (Honohan 2019: 3). It is not simply buying bonds, these asset-purchase programmes benefit homeowners, reinforcing the exclusion of households at the bottom of the income scale who are the worst affected because they are both non-bondholders and non-homeowners.

2.5   Asset-Based Inequality

The asset economy creates a specific structure of wealth creation via asset markets which are distributed unevenly across society. Therefore, the economic shock of the Covid-19 pandemic made inequality worse. As the UK Treasury Committee itself acknowledged, 'since households in the bottom half of the UK distribution hold little or no net wealth [assets], they have gained much less in absolute terms from growth in wealth than have families in higher deciles' (Treasury Select Committee 2021: 74). Figure 2.1 provides a breakdown of the composition, or forms, of wealth based on income decile in the UK from 2016 to 2018. To explain briefly: property wealth consists of valuations of any property owned by the household minus any loans or mortgages secured against the property. Physical wealth includes the value of household contents including antiques, artwork, and vehicles. Pension wealth is the value of occupational and personal pensions. Financial wealth includes the value of investments such as bank savings, stocks, and shares minus any financial liabilities. Business assets include the value of assets held within a business in which an individual is either self-employed or as a director or partner. They show the largest segment is private pension wealth (42%), followed closely by property wealth (35%). Financial wealth (15%) and physical wealth (9%) form the smaller portion each, respectively.

A major driver of the gains for wealthy families has been the fact that their financial portfolios contain a greater share of high yielding assets (see also Bach et al. 2020; Fagerend et al. 2020). The Wealth and Assets Survey (WAS) is the most comprehensive dataset available on household wealth in the UK, it shows that from 2016 to 18 the top three net wealth deciles held a larger share of wealth than they did 10 years earlier, and the middle 50% shrank; indeed, the top wealth deciles held 76% of all wealth in Great Britain, while the bottom deciles held only 2% (ONS 2018: 8). Financial assets are the most unequally distributed asset (91%) as ownership is concentrated at the top. Property and pension wealth are the

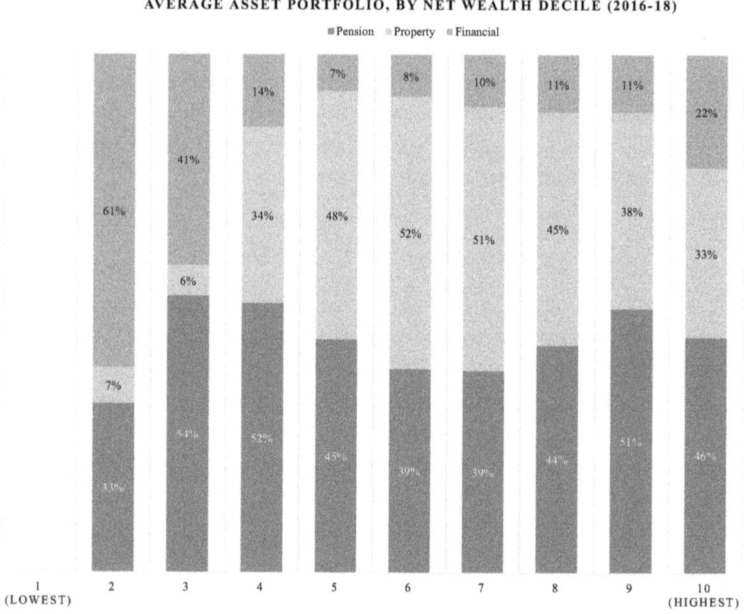

Fig. 2.1 UK composition and distribution of wealth (*Source* Wealth and Assets Survey 2016–18)

most common financial products owned by middle-income households—have Gini coefficients of 66% and 72%, respectively, which is indicating a high degree of inequality (ONS 2018: 7). What is most apparent from graph one is that wealth levels in the UK vary dramatically across the income distribution curve. The poorest 10% of families have negative net wealth—meaning that their debts exceed their assets, while the top 1% have almost £5 million per adult in the family (Wealth Tax Commission 2020: 11).

The top two deciles—the economic elite—are concentrated in the south-east of England with wealth holdings primarily in business and financial assets, and less dependent on income from property (houses) and physical wealth (vehicles and household contents) than lower income groups. Based on ONS estimates the top 10% of households have total assets of approximately £1 million, while entry into the 1% requires assets of £2.8 million (Dorling 2014: 95). In fact, the lower end of the 'rich' group has also seen—on average—wages stagnating, much as the middle group has. But we argue that it is still reasonable to place these top two deciles in a group with the super-rich 1%, because they are *more than simply* homeowners. Our central contention in this book is that the asset portfolios of the top two deciles has been one (if not, *the*) major determinant of their advantages during the pandemic.

For the remainder of this book we use a simple schema informed by the WAS analysis to divide households into three broad tranches: the top (the top two deciles, 9 and 10, from WAS), comprised of the wealthiest 20% of household in Great Britain; the middle (four middle deciles 5, 6, 7 and 8) as the numerical majority capturing both sides of the median, or mid-point; the bottom (deciles 1, 2, 3 and 4 from the WAS) encompasses all parts of the lower stratum of society, the working poor to those without formal income. These three groupings: the top, the middle, and the bottom are stylistic but also indicative of the three poles in UK society being driven further apart by the ascent of the asset economy.

2.6   The Fault Lines of Inequality

Having established the ascent of the asset economy and articulated how it is structured in the UK context, we turn now to the established fault lines of inequality in the UK which is the basis for our study of Covid-19 in subsequent chapters. Drawing on the existing understandings of financialisation of everyday life and the asset economy we position our evaluation of inequality within the existing literature, especially as it relates to the UK. Specifically, we tie together how the asset economy is connected to the growing concentration of wealth among those who already have assets holdings and the role of the state in promoting this trend, primarily through tax policy and promoting the 'democratisation' of assets. What is less well established is the specific impact of the asset economy in driving division in the UK and, the new fault lines of inequality which we map in this book. Asset ownership and the types of debt used dictate the types of state support provided—these are fault lines of inequality in the UK that divide the top, the middle, and the bottom of society.

What is important to draw out is how each social grouping has a recognisable relationship to asset markets, employment markets, and welfare provision of the state. This contrasts with University of Chicago economist, Raghuram Rajan's (2010) use of the term 'fault lines' to understand rising inequality as the outcome of economic structures (p. 4).

He postulates that the Greenspan era of low-interest rates and finance-driven growth in the US, and elsewhere among advanced economies, contributed to observable imbalances. Credit-driven and export-driven economies are competing in a globalised market creating fault lines; using a geological metaphor to explain how mixed economic systems create stress points (for instance, where tectonic plates collide). We want to preserve the focus on structural forces that generate inequality, but we diverge from Rajan's explanation of how 'these fault lines impact the financial sector' (p. 7). Unlike Rajan's metaphor, we develop an altogether different framing of the forces acting upon the UK economy that do not assimilate (erroneous) economic assumptions about what is inside (endogenous) and outside (exogenous). What Rajan sees as forces acting from outside (exogenous) we see as unfolding social forces in which the fault lines show only the effects. We contend that fault lines of inequality are reproduced by public policy that actively promotes the international financial architecture of the asset economy.

Thus, inequality results not just from the structure of national and global markets but is influenced by the role the state plays, via public policymaking. These dynamics create and sustain what we observe as social stratification. Of course, the influential work of Thomas Piketty (2014) is closely aligned to this book's recognition of government policies, namely taxation and inheritance laws, in configuring inequality across the arc of history. Piketty's use of historical evidence to track the fluctuations in income and wealth inequality across multiple countries provides the simple $\mathbf{r} > \mathbf{g}$ expression of inequality: where 'r' is the rate of return on capital and 'g' is the rate of growth in the economy, then inequality is when gains from growth accrue to asset owners compared to wage earners. For Piketty, returns on capital create gulfs between social strata, which are forged in and through differential taxation on income compared to capital. His substantive book makes a simple, yet highly persuasive argument for economists, that income and wealth inequality are the product of the division of national capital; what eminent economist Robert Solow labelled the 'rich-get-richer dynamic' (see Solow 1974). In other words: the fault line of inequality is established between whether you get your income from work or from investments. Why this is important is because it imposes clear structural restraints, making equality of opportunity impossible.

However, as Adkins et al. (2020: 37) point out, a purely economic understanding of inequality, like those put forward by Piketty, Solow and Stiglitz, offer only a simple critique or rentierism. The rentier is an economic term referring to those that earn 'unearned' income and has been a persistent point of economic debate since Adam Smith right up to the 1950s Cambridge Capital Controversies. Why this is relevant here is because focusing exclusively on how income is generated from 'capital' leads only to ways of conceptualising the composition of income and wealth, not inequality itself—which conceptualises whom in society has capital and who does not. What Adkins et al., point out is that rentierism also does not capture social stratifications, nor how the logics of the asset economy transform society in ways that generate inequality.

Admittedly, there are many critiques of Piketty and rentierism. For instance, critics have pointed out that his work lacks an understanding of class conflict in its framing of 'capital' (Mongiovi 2015), and it completely neglects inequality in terms of gender, race and other stratifications (Eisenstein 2014). This fits within a wider critique of the economics bias towards system stabilisation, rather than egalitarian concerns (Nunn 2015), which never generates sufficiently robust explanations of why inequality should rise or fall (Harvey 2014). Our focus on public policy pushes at this tension. While Piketty is concerned with 'highlighting patterns of increasing inequality of income and wealth' rather than analysing the ways in which these are 'generated from unequal and dynamic social relations' we believe we are showing, in contrast to Piketty, how they are 'enforced by ....state strategies' (Nunn 2015: 4). Thus, the focus on state strategies means digging into UK policy responses to the Covid-19 pandemic to examine how inequality is impacted.

We argue that moving beyond strictly national macroeconomic framings of inequality is crucial and necessary for recognising how the asset economy shapes the fault lines of inequality. Following Oxford economist Anthony Atkinson's expansive book (2015), *Inequality: what can be done?* we locate rising inequality as fundamentally about distribution within national economies and globally. Atkinson frames inequality as having many dimensions (p. 28): income, class, gender, and generation, and clearly outlines how key trends such as globalisation, technology, financialisation, wage stagnation, reduced power of trade unions, and welfare state retrenchment each contributed to widening inequality. We take from Atkinson the explicit view that inequality is not 'exogenous' to the economic and social system. An example from the book is 'globalisation' often portrayed as the march of corporate capital around the globe was in fact a result of decisions taken by international organisations, by national governments, by corporations, and by individuals' (p. 82). Indeed, what is most relevant is that the periods during which inequality has fallen have been shown to occur because of more effective redistribution policies by the state.

As it pertains to the UK case explicitly, there is also the work of Stuart Lansley (2012) and Danny Dorling (2014), each coming from a slightly different vantage point examining income and wealth inequality in the UK and the role played by public policy to enable it. Lansley focuses on the public policy agenda since Thatcher which initiated financial liberalisation, detailing how successive UK governments promoted capital over income gains, while rolling back on key elements of the post-war universal welfare state which all contributed to widening inequality. For Dorling, the political power of the wealthiest 1% of households is what makes the UK a 'class society'. He starts with stratifications of income and wealth inequality and goes on to show how they are reproduced through recognisable policy agendas in education, employment, and housing.

We wish to add to this literature on UK inequality by specifically focusing on the Covid-19 pandemic response and what happened to inequality trends as a result. We integrate this existing literature to articulate the fault lines of inequality in relation to the stratifications of society. Adapting Adkins's (2019: 5) argument that 'the key element shaping inequality is whether one is able to buy assets that appreciate at a faster rate than both inflation and wages' we further elaborate on how this impacts the three trenches top, middle, bottom—in specific ways. Thus, accepting the connections the three trenches of society have to specific assets is necessary to evaluate who benefited from Covid-19 economic response packages, and who did not.

Figure 2.2 provides a simple artist's impression of how we understand the new fault lines at the heart of the UK economy. State managers begin with the premise that access to markets and possession of assets is the 'goose which lays the golden egg'. Put crudely, this premise shapes how government policymakers manage and distribute economic resources. Those groups in society with asset-holdings (those at the top) reap first-order benefits because their assets automatically gain value: their house prices rise; their investments produce dividends and gain value; and their pension pots increase. In the event of economic turmoil those with assets are protected, via bailouts which act as public safety nets either through central-bank interventions in financial markets or the defence of commercial and domestic property ownership. Government intervention to put a

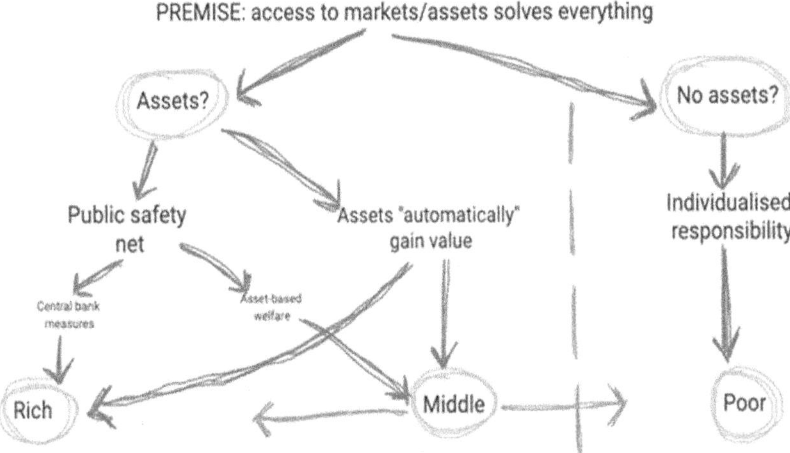

Fig. 2.2 The new fault lines of inequality (Authors impression)

floor under asset-market losses is 'socialism' for the rich. Thus, the already wealthy at the top are the main beneficiaries of asset gains in good times and bailouts in bad times, because of the range of assets, they hold, and the government support attached to them.

Those in the middle have limited asset-holdings, overwhelmingly their primary residence and some portfolio investment (such as pensions), which puts them in a more fragile position. Their assets gain value (such as house-price rises) and they receive certain public support during times of crisis, through state enforcement of mortgage payment holidays and furlough packages for example, in the case of Covid-19. The economic experiences of the middle are highly insecure though. On paper the middle is asset rich (through home ownership and housing equity) and therefore recipients of government asset-based welfare support. While their lived experiences are far closer to those of the working poor. They are often exposed to the same financial and psychological stresses; they are often cash poor with low levels of disposable income and levels of household debt. For example, a considerable proportion of those receiving three-day emergency food packages during the pandemic came from middle-income households.

The common identity and interest of the middle is also fractured. The individualism which affects the poor and the rich (albeit in hugely diverse ways) also harms the middle because their situation is both precarious and fragile. They are torn between being psychologically and practically attached to their home (Schwartz and Seabrooke 2008) and tormented by the disciplining effect of the asset economy (Bonefeld 1995). Their asset, their home, is—at the same time—their liberation and their prison. Their house is their means of survival, the source of their wealth, and their financial precarity.

The bottom of the distribution, or the poor, have no assets. They rely only on low-paid work and government support to survive. The structure of the asset economy ensures those at the bottom do not reap the gains of automatic rises in asset values; over a decade of austerity ensures they receive little in the way of government support. The overriding message is that they are responsible for their own welfare and well-being, rather than in receipt of collective (or universal) welfare provision. This means that during peace times those on low incomes live hand-to-mouth, while in times of (national) economic crisis they face a daily life or death struggle to survive.

2.7   Closing Thoughts

This chapter examined the fault lines of inequality in the UK in income and wealth terms, which informs the basis of our analysis of Covid-19 economic responses in subsequent chapters. We trace how financialisation in the UK economy contributed to rising inequality, we focus on how public policy shaped the UK's economic model since the 1980s. The unacknowledged policy regime of privatised Keynesianism and asset-based welfare gave rise to the asset economy; we pay close attention to how public policy shapes the integration of finance into everyday life. We argue, which is the major contribution of our analysis, that the growing prominence of incomes from assets and the complicated role of debt forge deeper divisions between the top, the middle, and the bottom—as key social strata we map throughout the book.

References

Adkins, L. 2019. Social reproduction in the neoliberal era: Payments, leverage and the Minskian household. *Polygraph* 27: 19–33.
Adkins, L., M. Cooper, and M. Konings. 2020. *The asset economy*. Wiley.

Adkins, L., M. Cooper, and M. Konings. 2021. Class in the 21st century: Asset inflation and the new logic of inequality. *Environment and Planning A: Economy and Space* 53 (3): 548–572.

Atkinson, A.B. 2015. *Inequality: What can be done?* Harvard University Press.

Bach, L., et al. 2020. Rich pickings? Risk, return, and skill in household wealth. *American Economic Review* 110 (9): 2703–2747.

Bank of England. 2020. Quantitative easing—Fact sheet, gov.co.uk, November. Available at: https://www.bankofengland.co.uk/monetary-policy/quantitat ive-easing. Accessed 12 November 2021.

Beck, Roland, et al. 2019. Medium-term treatment and side-effects of quantitative easing: International evidence. ECB Working Paper No. 2229.

Best, J. 2005. *The limits of transparency: Ambiguity and the history of international finance.* Ithaca, New York: Cornell University Press.

Bonefeld, W. 1995. The Politics of Debt: Social discipline and control. *Common Sense* 17: 69–91.

Brookings. 2015. Kevin Warsh, Don Kohn on QE and inequality, 10 June.

Bump, P. 2013. Obama calls inequality the "defining challenge of our time." *The Atlantic*, 4 December.

Christophers, B. 2020. *Rentier capitalism: Who owns the economy, and who pays for it?* Verso Books.

Dorling, D. 2014. *Inequality and the 1%*. London and New York: Verso Books.

Dorling, D. 2019. *Inequality and the 1%*, 2nd ed. London and New York: Verso Books.

Eisenstein, Z. 2014. *Hatreds: Racialized and sexualised conflicts in the 21st century*. New York: Routledge.

Epstein, G.A. 2005. Introduction. In *Financialization and the world economy: A reader*, ed. G.A. Epstein. Cheltenham: Edward Elgar.

Fagereng, A., et al. 2020. Heterogeneity and persistence in returns to wealth. *Econometrica* 88 (1): 115–170.

Financial Times. 2015. Four reasons why QE will be different in the eurozone, 20 January.

Forbes. 2015. How Federal Reserve Quantitative Easing Expanded Wealth Inequality, 25 June.

Froud, J., S. Johal, C. Haslam, and K. Williams. 2001. Accumulation under conditions of inequality. *Review of International Political Economy* 8 (1): 66–95.

Giles, C. 2016. UK suffering 'first lost decade since 1860s' says Carney. *Financial Times*, 5 December. Available at: https://www.ft.com/content/c0c36268-bb0d-11e6-8b45-b8b81dd5d080. Accessed 16 March 2022.

Harvey, D. 2014. Afterthoughts on Piketty's Capital. http://davidharvey.org/2014/05.

Hay, C. 2009. Good inflation, bad inflation: The housing boom, economic growth and the disaggregation of inflationary preferences in the UK and Ireland. *The British Journal of Politics & International Relations* 11 (3): 461–478.

Hay, C. 2011. Pathology without crisis? The strange demise of the Anglo-Liberal growth model. *Government and Opposition* 46 (1): 1–31.

Hohberger, S., R. Priftis, and L. Vogel. 2019. The macroeconomic effects of quantitative easing in the euro area: Evidence from an estimated DSGE model. *Journal of Economic Dynamics and Control* 108: 103756. https://doi.org/10.1016/j.jedc.2019.103756.

Honohan, P. 2019. Should Monetary Policy Take Inequality and Climate Change into Account?

IFS. 2020. Trends in Economic Inequality. The IFS Deaton Review.

Krippner, G.R. 2011. *Capitalizing on crisis: The political origins of the rise of finance*. Cambridge, MA: Harvard University Press.

Kuznets, S. 1955. Economic growth and income inequality. *The American Economic Review, American Economic Association* 45 (1): 1–28.

Lansley, S. 2012. *The cost of inequality: Why equality is essential for recovery*. Gibson Square.

Lazonick, W., and M. O'Sullivan. 2000. Maximizing shareholder value: A new ideology for corporate governance. *Economy and Society* 29 (1): 13–35.

Lowe, S.G., B.A. Searle, and S.J. Smith. 2012. from housing wealth to mortgage debt: The emergence of Britain's asset-shaped welfare state. *Social Policy and Society* 11 (1): 105–116.

Malpass, P. 2008. Housing and the New Welfare State: Wobbly pillar or cornerstone? *Housing Studies* 23 (1): 1–19.

Mongiovi, G. 2015. Piketty on capitalism and inequality: A radical economics perspective. *Review of Radical Political Economics* 47 (4): 558–565.

Macartney, H. 2019. *The bank culture debate: Ethics, values and financialisation in Anglo-America*. Oxford University Press.

NBER. 2020. Fifty Shades of QE: Comparing findings of central bankers and academics. NBER Working Papers 27849.

Nunn, A. 2015. Unpicking Piketty's Problems: The Production and Reproduction of Inequality in Times of Austerity, Paper to ESRC Workshop, London, December.

ONS. 2018. Total Wealth in Great Britain: April 2016 to March 2018. Available at: https://www.ons.gov.uk/peoplepopulationandcommunity/personalandhouseholdfinances/incomeandwealth/bulletins/totalwealthingreatbritain/april2016tomarch2018. Accessed 17 November 2021.

Pickett, K. 2019. What's the best way to tackle health inequalities? In *Rethinking Britain: Policy Ideas for the Many*, ed. S. Konzelmann, S. Himmelweit, J. Smith, and J. Weeks, 198–201. London: Policy Press.

Pickett, K., and R. Wilkinson. 2010. *The Spirit Level: Why Equality Is Better for Everyone*. Penguin UK.

Piketty, T. 2014. *Capital in the Twenty-First Century*, trans. A. Goldhammer. Cambridge, MA: Harvard University Press.

Rajan, R. 2010. *Fault lines: How hidden fractures still threaten the world economy*, Vol. New ed. Princeton, NJ: Princeton University Press, Woodstock.

Ronald, L., et al. 2017. Whatever happened to asset-based welfare? *Shifting Approaches to Housing Wealth and Welfare Security, Policy and Politics* 45 (2): 173–193.

Ronald, R. 2008. *The ideology of home ownership: Homeowner societies and the role of housing*. New York: Palgrave Macmillan, Basingstoke.

Ronald, R., and M. Elsinga, eds. 2012. *Beyond Home Ownership: Housing, Welfare and Society*. London: Routledge.

Savage, M. 2021. *The return of inequality: Social change and the weight of the past*. Harvard University Press.

Schwartz, H., and L. Seabrooke. 2008. Varieties of residential capitalism in the international political economy: Old welfare states and the new politics of housing. *Comparative European Politics* 6 (2): 237–261.

Solow, R.M. 1974. Intergenerational equity and exhaustible resources. *The Review of Economic Studies* [Oxford University Press, Review of Economic Studies, Ltd.] 41: 29–45.

Streeck, W. 2014. *Buying time: The delayed crisis of democratic capitalism*. Verso Books.

Syll, L. 2014. Piketty and the limits of marginal productivity theory. *Real World Economics Review* 69: 36–43.

Toussaint, J., and M. Elsinga. 2009. Exploring 'housing asset-based welfare': Can the UK be held up as an example for Europe? *Housing Studies* 24 (5): 669–692.

UK Parliament. 2020. Income Inequality in the UK: Research briefing, 13 August.

Watson, M. 2009. Headlong into the Polanyian Dilemma: The impact of middle-class moral panic on the British Government's response to the sub-prime crisis. *British Journal of Politics and International Relations* 11 (3): 422–437.

Wealth Tax Commission. 2020. Final report of the wealth tax commission, 9 December 2020. Wealth Tax Commission.

Williamson, S.D. 2017. Quantitative easing: How well does this tool work? Federal Reserve Bank of St Louis, Regional Economist Q3.

WSJ. 2020. Derby's Take: New research says central bank view on bond buying too rosey, 29 September.

CHAPTER 3

A Windfall at the Top

Abstract This chapter argues that—in large part as a result of the monetary policy interventions by central banks and the protections of non-reforms of fiscal policy—the wealth of the richest increased during the pandemic. These policy responses followed the established post-crisis template of the asset economy, offering an unlimited safety net to holders of financial assets via central-bank quantitative easing and inflation-targeting initiatives; at the same time, as—inter alia—private pensions and capital gains were threatened by political and economic pressures, non-interventions by the Treasury insulated the wealthiest members of society. In particular though, we argue that the "blank cheque" written for financial asset holders stands in stark contrast to the (indefensible) meagre and time-limited efforts to assist the poorest in society through the pandemic. In this chapter, we trace the monetary and fiscal policy interventions that benefited the three main asset classes of the rich—financial investments, property, and private pensions—thereby contributing to rising inequality.

Keywords Monetary policy · Fiscal policy · Pensions · Property · Investments

H. Macartney et al., *The Fault Lines of Inequality*, https://doi.org/10.1007/978-3-030-96914-1_3

37

3.1   Introduction

The UK's privatised Keynesianism policy regime promotes an asset economy that drives the fault lines of inequality that divide the top, the middle, and the bottom of society. Traditional measures of income inequality—to differentiate between different groups in society—isolate the employment market as the sole generator of inequality related to wage levels from different jobs. For example, certain jobs earn much higher wages and salaries than others which is why incomes are unequal. However, to understand the very 'top' of the distribution, income from employment is less relevant, income from assets, or wealth inequality, is the chasm between social strata.

Our claim is that the widening of the gap between the top (the 'rich') and the bottom (the 'poor') has less to do with income from wages and more to do with income from assets. As such it builds upon the Resolution Foundation (2021) Wealth Gap Year report which highlights that the most important driver of wealth gains during the pandemic was asset-price increases (p. 31). Their estimates suggest that of the £890bn increase in total wealth (combined savings and asset-price increases), changes in asset prices account for the majority (£765bn). As a result of their asset ownership, 'the richest households have [therefore] seen the largest wealth increases' as Covid-19 unfolded (ibid.). This chapter charts the fate of those at the top.

Determining who "belongs" to this wealthiest group is no mean feat though. There are clear gender dynamics to wealth concentration before and during the Covid-19 pandemic. As Tracey Warren (2006) finds, the gender distribution of pension wealth is much more skewed than for total wealth, with women owning only 29% of pension wealth but 44% of total wealth. This partly reflects the fact that a much smaller share of women (66%) has access to pensions, compared to 100% of men (12). Deere and Doss's (2006) article 'The Gender Asset Gap' also details the distribution of asset ownership within the household through the legal structures and institutions that regulate the ownership of assets within marriage and inheritance regimes and its relative impact on women's access to wealth and own assets. Overall, there is a significant gender gap in total wealth in the UK, and it favours men. The wealthiest in society are overwhelmingly male and mostly white, the rest of society is conspicuous in their exclusion.

Similarly, racialised forms of inequality are based on a collection of structural forces that cumulatively create conditions of deprivation. Indeed, following Marsa Bardaradan's rich study of the racial wealth gap in the US, *The Color of Money*, we must acknowledge how—overlapping forms of financial exploitation—leave people of colour without capital in a capitalist country. A follow-on, UK specific analysis by Omar Khan (2020) details how People from Black and Ethnic Minority Backgrounds in the UK generally have much lower levels of savings or assets than White British people: while Indian households have 90–95p for every £1 of White British wealth, Pakistani households have around 50p, Black Caribbean around 20p, and Black African and Bangladeshi approximately 10p.

Therefore, when discussing how the wealthiest in the UK fared during the pandemic it is not simply about the individuals, households, or dynasties that accumulated more wealth; it is also about who was systemically excluded from it. That being said, a key message of this chapter is not only that the wealth of the richest increased significantly as a product of state policy interventions, but that the wealthiest—in general—had far better *lived* experiences of the pandemic than those at the bottom.

On this latter point, in July 2020, the Evening Standard Insider published an exposé on Paracelsus Recovery, the exclusive rehabilitation centre in Switzerland, entitled '*How the 1% struggled to cope with the lockdown*'. The seven-star, luxury centre is renowned for assigning a 15-strong team of doctors and therapists to only one client at a time. During the pandemic Paracelsus explained that they had seen calls and referrals 'skyrocket', claiming that they had 'never had such a huge number of calls at one time' (*Evening Standard* 2020). Their clientele—ranging from CEOs to heads of state, and royalty to Hollywood A-listers—had approached the centre as a result of the loneliness and alcoholism caused by repeated national lockdowns. The £65,000 per week costs though reflected the simple fact that the mega-rich 0.1% had a vastly dissimilar experience of the Covid-19 pandemic to those of the other 99.9%.

Indeed, in eight out of the ten countries represented by the Credit Suisse Wealth Report (2021: 24), the wealth share of the top 1% increased in 2020. In fact, the Report was damning in its conclusion: 'regarding what happened in 2020, the verdict is unanimous. The indices all agree that global wealth inequality rose in 2020 by a substantial amount'; and 'the inequality rise in 2020 was significantly greater than that recorded in any year this century' (ibid.). By 2022 then the Office of National Statistics (ONS) reported that the wealth of the richest 1% of households was more than 230 times that of the poorest 10% (*The Independent* 2022). The majority of the (initial) fall and subsequent gains in wealth occurred during 2020 and the first part of 2021, so our analysis focuses on the politics of this period. The purpose is to contextualise these wind-fall gains within the established fault lines of inequality.

Finally, this all points towards the political message which we elaborate in our closing chapter, because there is a clear ethical tension in that the outbreak of the Covid-19 pandemic led to windfall gains at the top of the distribution, while economic hardship is widespread in large swathes of the economy.

3.2   Governing the Asset Economy

At the outbreak of a financial crisis, the state will tend to step in to prevent market failure from becoming a total system collapse. A basic template for economic recovery after a crisis has emerged since the 1980s—from Black Wednesday, the East Asian Crisis, the 2008 global financial crisis, and then Covid. Each iteration of crisis deploys (minimal) Treasury fiscal measures and (expansive) Bank of England monetary measures to respond to events rather than deal with their causes.

To unpack the structural drivers of inequalities in income and wealth, we focus on these two specific policy mechanisms—fiscal policy and monetary policy—as connection points between the state and the asset economy. Examining these policy mechanisms is done to put forward the claim that those at the top, or the richest in society, benefitted to such an extent that it has further widened the fault lines, or chasms, between the top, the middle, and the bottom social strata.

Specifically, the economic crisis response measures did the utmost to defend the wealth of asset owners: the Bank of England's monetary policy kept asset prices up, while fiscal measures were emergency and temporary, and often limited to targeting middle-income households. This response only generates stagnation, as the closer interest rates get to the zero lower bound (0%) the less effective central-bank monetary policy is at stimulating the economy (Wren-Lewis 2014); while at the same time (any, albeit meagre) fiscal measures become a justification for austerity in the future. This will only serve to compound inequality and stagnation further as it did post-2008, when fiscal constraint was imposed too soon (Boyer 2012; Montgomerie 2016).

3.2.1 Monetary Policy—How Central Banks Defend Asset Owners

The most important economic policy measures affecting wealth gains were central-bank monetary policy interventions (Resolution Foundation 2021: 32). In 2020, the Covid-19 pandemic induced substantial market instability that threatened the wealth of asset owners. Market panics and manias are a chronic feature of a finance-driven asset economy, and a deadly virus circulating the globe posed a unique threat to global production networks as much as financial markets. The initial collapse in asset markets in early 2020 was extreme. From 24th February the UK's FTSE 100 slumped by approximately 8%, or £152 billion, in a week (*The Guardian* 2020a). Initial BoE measures were sizeable because—as the new Governor of the Bank of England (Andrew Bailey) noted—studies had suggested that going 'big and fast is particularly effective during periods of market illiquidity' (BoE 2020b). Once market functioning had normalised by July 2020, central banks and governments reduced the pace of their support measures.

While equities markets in the UK have only recently returned to pre-pandemic levels, global equities in general had risen over 20% by the end of 2021 (Resolution Foundation 2021: 33). The various forms of wealth multiplication for the rich were therefore closely connected to the actions taken by central banks and governments to (ostensibly) promote recovery of financial markets in 2020. The most recent Credit Suisse Wealth Report (2021: 24) highlighted, 'the rise in wealth inequality was likely not caused by the pandemic itself, nor its direct economic impacts, but was instead a consequence of actions undertaken to mitigate its impact' by state policymakers. In media reporting it was pointed out, 'governments and central banks have stepped in with huge fiscal and monetary interventions that have sustained, and in many cases added to, the fortunes of the wealthy' (*The Guardian* 2021a). Surprisingly, the potential linkages between monetary policy and inequality were even widely acknowledged, especially as it became clear that existing areas of deprivation were also hardest hit by the Covid-19 infections, illness, and death.

While unprecedented interventions by state policymakers saved the UK economy from collapse, it did so by making inequality much worse by allowing for windfall gains for asset owners. The tension here is that expanding the bank reserves (by the central bank) and the racking up of debt (by the government) to defend financial markets and asset owners are presented as a good and necessary investment. Generous rounds of monetary financing and bond-buying led one commentator to conclude 'there is a permanent welfare safety net for financial markets' (*The Guardian* 2020a). Favouring asset owners and abandoning non-asset owners, or those that rely on wage income, causes extreme pressure that drives the poles between them further apart during a period of extreme human suffering. Supporting the already wealthy, compares here to the abandonment of those without assets, whose misfortune is an atrocity of breath-taking proportions. This is particularly true when you compare the government and central-bank claim that 'we're prepared to do everything it takes' to save financial markets and asset owners, compared with the narrative of 'there's no money left in the kitty' to provide—inter alia—free school meals during holidays for deprived children.

From the moment it was clear that coronavirus was of global concern the Bank of England took immediate and unprecedented action. On 11th March, the BoE's three policy committees announced a package of monetary measures because 'asset and commodity prices [had] fallen sharply', suggesting that 'indicators of financial market uncertainty [had] reached extreme lows' (BoE 2020b). Then, on 19 March 2020 a special meeting of the MPC was held to vote on a further package of central-bank measures buying £870 billion of UK government bonds and sterling non-financial investment-grade corporate bonds for £200 billion, as well as reducing the base interest rate to 0.1% (BoE 2020c). Taken together as (un)conventional monetary policy—interest-rate reduction, Quantitative Easing (QE), and asset-purchase programme—were the immediate crisis response template. The macro-prudential policy coordination mechanism between the Treasury and the BoE acted decisively to support the asset economy. As is typical, the rationale for this template is the belief that state-backed funds in circulation will stimulate the economy 'reflating it with new investment and employment' (Hedrick-Wong 2015). In reality though, bond purchasing programmes had done more to inflate asset prices than to generate economic growth and recovery since 2008; thus, we can expect the same generalised 'secular' stagnation to result from this round of monetary policy.

Monetary crisis response measures are designed to be timely and powerful interventions by the state into markets. A package of measures—from cutting the base interest rate, lowering private banks' capital buffers, and offering cheap funding to the banks—are designed to generate macroeconomic stability and recovery. Namely by sending a signal to banks to lend to households and businesses to generate investment and consumption that creates economic growth. In the words of Jonathan Haskel, a member of the BoE MPC, 'the first round of purchases aimed to prevent and stop in its tracks the financial market dysfunction resulting from the significant ...adjustment that occurred at the onset of this crisis in March' (BoE 2020d: 1). To the naked eye monetary measures were designed 'to support business and consumer confidence at a challenging time... and to improve the availability of finance', rather than directly targeting asset owners (Mark Carney, former governor of the BoE, cited in FT 2020b). Critics swiftly pointed out, however, that cutting borrowing costs by a few basis points would have minimal benefits for struggling businesses, though the measures would 'help to support confidence in the markets... which [had] taken a severe knock' (chief economist at the Institute of Directors, cited in FT 2020c). And this is the recurrent theme, the rhetoric of 'helping businesses and households bridge across the economic disruption' (BoE 2020b) should be interpreted as insulating asset owners from the effects of the pandemic, which has significant impacts on levels of inequality.

By June however, the immediate period of market turmoil was easing, and this led to the second wave of BoE measures. In this second phase, the Bank slowed the pace at which it would inject money by 2/3 compared to the period from March to June (FT 2020c). Again though, it would be a mistake to overlook the sheer scale of the Bank of England spending packages even when reduced and to not contrast it with government efforts to help the poor.

Apart from these differences in support, we cannot neglect that the BoE's interventions have been instrumental in improving market conditions (FT 2020a). At one point it was reported the BoE pandemic response was so intense it was purchasing £4.5 billion per week until the end of 2020, leading to criticism the central bank was permanently financing government debt (Whittaker 2020). In other words, pumping cash into the financial system reduced investors' fears about the liquidity of markets in general. For the purposes of our argument though, these interventions were specifically focused on government bonds which supported particularly asset prices from falling. The greater the market volatility, the greater the threat to asset prices, hence BoE monetary measures were <u>the</u> saving grace for asset owners exposed to losses due to the outbreak of the Covid-19 pandemic.

After the summer of 2020, policy interventions shifted to giving guidance on the pace and timing of withdrawing the crisis response measures before inflation and stagnation set in. These too revealed that the asset economy was at the forefront of macroeconomic and monetary policy planning. Traditionally, monetary measures were based on an inverse correlation between stocks and government bonds so that when corporate earnings fell and stock prices came under pressure, central banks would cut interest rates; and the fall in interest rates would raise government bond prices. This meant that—in the past—investors with a balanced portfolio would weather these cycles.

Unconventional monetary policy had changed the rules of the game though. Now, 'everything [had] gone up – stocks, credit and core bond prices' (FT 2020d). This was an important point to note because on the one hand, it meant that the post-2008 crisis intervention had boosted asset prices across the board; but it also meant that the way in which the central banks chose to withdraw or scale-back asset purchasing programmes would also have major repercussions. Even moderate investors would be hit if central banks chose to withdraw support for government bonds, credit, and stocks at the same time (Reuters 2022).

With these new 'rules of the game' in mind it was significant that in August 2020 the Bank issued two types of forward guidance, both of which insulated asset owners. Firstly, it would delay tightening monetary policy until inflation had risen quite dramatically (FT 2020e); and secondly, it would gradually wind down QE in a way that created space for further bond-buying measures if conditions worsened. The Bank reiterated that 'it stood ready to increase the pace of [bond] purchases' if required by market conditions (BoE 2020f). As Governor Bailey explained to the Jackson Hole conference of central bankers, the BoE aimed to 'ensure there is sufficient headroom for more potent expansion in central bank balance sheets when needed in the future – to "go big" and "go fast" decisively' (BoE 2020e). Most striking is the persistent 'do whatever it takes message' to protect financial markets and asset owners from losses. By extension, this also means that the BoE had effectively written a blank cheque for the UK government by committing to further debt monetisation.

This willingness to 'go big' was again visible as the economic recovery slowed by the autumn of 2020 and the BoE further extended its QE programme by £150 billion, to stave off any further uncertainty. Governor Bailey and MPC Member Sir Dave Ramsden emphasised that 'the policy environment has evolved a huge amount' and so 'thinking about headroom [the limits to QE programmes] has evolved really significantly' (cited in BoE 2020a: 3). This was a politically correct way of saying that there was in fact no upper limit to central-bank spending to defend markets, which directly benefits only asset owners. The importance of this messaging should therefore not be overlooked. The Bank was subtly reassuring observers that its price stability, inflation-targeting mandate remained front and centre in its policy planning. A monetary policy mandate was being articulated, with the interests of asset holders at the forefront.

In terms of our argument about how public policy choices have a direct impact on wealth and inequality, the BoE played an instrumental role in protecting asset prices which directly benefits the already wealthy. This was particularly clear by the third and fourth quarters of 2021, as inflation rose by 4.6% from 12 months earlier. But it quickly became apparent that the two features of the Bank of England's monetary policy response held firm: the Bank had promised to tighten policy slowly; and markets seemed convinced by the Bank's promises to defend asset prices.

On the first, while other central banks (including the US Federal Reserve) began reining back their asset-purchase programmes, the Bank of England only made modest changes to its interest rate, raising it to 0.25%. It also clarified that it would not begin "unwinding" (selling off assets) the Quantitative Easing programmes until interest rates reached 1%; and independent analysis by the Office of Budgetary Responsibility late in 2021 forecast that rates would not reach that level until at least 2027 (OBR 2021: 29–30).

While on the second issue, despite concerns about the massive ($36tn) increase in global debt since the start of the pandemic and the potential for an asset-price bubble to burst (GMO 2021), the lack of massive sell-offs by investors suggested that the Bank of England signalling had been effective (FT 2022). Investors seemed to be anticipating 'accommodative monetary conditions and zero real rates going on indefinitely' (ibid.).

Thus by December 2021 it was clear that the actions of central banks had proven effective: the MSCI world index of developed market shares had risen 16% in 2020 and 22% in 2021 (MSCI 2022). As we will see later in this chapter this global recovery boosted the financial assets of the top echelons. In terms of our argument about the increase in wealth and inequality as a product of policies pursued by the British state, the Bank of England had played an instrumental role in this growth in asset prices. It had helped fund the government, stabilise markets, and protect the accumulated wealth of the rich.

3.2.2   *Fiscal Policy—Taxation as Driver of Inequality*

It was not simply central-bank measures that affected wealth inequality though. Fiscal policy (non-)decisions also played an important role. Traditional understandings of state managers' allocation function focus on the Treasury policies of taxation and spending, or fiscal policy measures. As we detailed last chapter, Piketty's (2014) book used historical tax records to connect state taxation policy with the expansion or contraction of income inequality over time. A more recent detailed analysis of OECD countries' tax policies by Hope and Lindberg (2022) concurs, 'our analysis finds strong evidence that cutting taxes on the rich increases income inequality but has no effect on growth or unemployment' (2). Therefore, we take as our starting point that the UK Treasury's tax and spend, or fiscal policy, is contributing to worsening inequality.

Our argument is not that these fiscal measures added additional value to the assets of the rich, but that they protected them from further losses at a time when those assets were vulnerable to financial and political threats. Two of the most obvious measures were non-reforms to capital gains tax (affecting financial assets) and non-reforms of inflation measures—affecting pensions.

The structure of the UK economy, particularly as it pertains to the idiosyncrasies of the tax system, became a critical issue as the debate about paying for the Covid interventions developed. Our focus is on how these two policy branches created intervention measures that contributed to worsening inequality. When it comes to those at the top the most important policy is 'taxation' because the structure of the tax system itself played a significant role in creating wealth inequality before the pandemic struck. UK tax policy contributes to rising inequality between asset owners and the rest, by taking income earned from employment (income tax) or income earned from sales of goods and services (value-added tax) compared to much lower tax rates on income from assets (capital gains) or investment (carried interest). The Centre for Economic Justice argued in 2021 that the underlying structure of the economy, by which they meant primarily the emphasis on asset ownership and the tax regime applied to the rich, had continued 'to funnel wealth and power to the richest in society' (*The Independent* 2021).

The reluctance of UK state policymakers to take steps to redress widening inequality resulting from the tax system compounded the wealth gap by insulating asset owners from losses during the pandemic (Tax Justice UK 2022). The tax system is effectively weighted in favour of the rich, defending their wealth. A University of Warwick report (2020) highlighted, 'where you get your money from (or at least how you package it) matters, because investment income and capital gains are taxed at lower rates than income from work'. Part of the challenge, related to the structure of the economy, is that even among the top 1% of income earners there remained a huge amount of diversity in real tax burdens. Only one in four of those higher income earners pay the official, top rate of 45% income tax, while one in ten pays only 11% (University of Warwick 2020). Meanwhile capital gains are more lightly taxed than income, with rates varying between 10 and 28% depending on the type of asset. By contrast, the top 0.01% accrue more than half of the benefits of these lower tax rates, because the vast majority of those within the top 1% receive almost 95% of their remuneration each year in the form of taxable income rather than capital gains (ibid: 11). Therefore, inequality is worsening because of the asset economy; those that earn income from assets keep more of it for themselves, while those that earn income from employment must pay a higher rate of taxation. For example, the average person with total remuneration of £10 million has an effective tax rate of just 21% (ibid.: 2) Thus 'with a deft sleight of hand, wealthy individuals can take large amounts of their earnings in the form of shares or other assets to avoid it being taxed as income' (*The Guardian* 2020d, see Resolution Foundation 2020 for a comprehensive summary).

To put it simply, the structure of the UK's asset economy is deeply connected to the Treasury's taxation system which is heavily weighted in favour of those who receive money from sources other than their wages. Yet, UK policymakers continued to turn a "blind eye" to this problem during the pandemic. Early in 2020 the Office of Tax Simplification recommended reforms to Capital Gains Tax (CGT) to bring it into alignment with income tax rates. The potential revenues raised by CGT reform were disputed—with critics arguing that since CGT was a 'voluntary tax, if rates increase… it would be difficult to predict what the revenue increase would be' (CityWire 2020). The basic criticism is that wealthy people are the 'important minority' which would be negatively affected by CGT reform and would, in turn, create negative impacts on wider society as the wealthy then choose to 'sit on their assets' rather than to pay a higher rate of tax. By October 2021, analysis of the 540,000 wealthiest individuals in the UK showed that if tax rates on shares and property were brought into line with taxes on salaries the government could raise an additional £16bn (*The Guardian* 2021b). Government reluctance to introduce CGT reforms simply reinforced the structural bias within the UK tax system towards owners of assets over wage earners.

Another important example of how policymakers impacted daily life in the pandemic was the technocratic practice of indexing of government support payments, like pensions and universal credit, but also government-backed student loans. During Covid-19, the UK government protected the wealth of the rich by delaying changes to the measurement of inflation which would have impacted private pensioners and bondholders (asset owners) negatively. The simplest explanation is that there are two measures of price change which are based on different baskets of goods, this translates into the retail prices index (RPI) and consumer prices index (CPI). Over time, the trend is clear with the higher rate of RPI change tending to favour pensioners and bondholders; and the lower rate of CPI change favouring, in general, creditors and debt-securities holders. That the government uses different ways of measuring price changes is a dull and technocratic observation, but how these measures are applied by policymakers has concrete social outcomes.

Before the pandemic struck, in September 2019 the UK Statistics Authority demanded that the British Chancellor switch from RPI to CPI measures, arguing that it provided a more accurate measure of price changes in the national economy. As it turns out, this small change would have reduced the value of government bonds by approximately £100 billion, in turn severely impacting private pension schemes. After extensive criticism of the RPI measure it became untenable for the British Chancellor to resist reform. But most commentators had expected the changes to be announced in 2020 and formally introduced by the time of the April 2021 Budget. Instead, in a move which was seen by critics to be insulating older asset owners and holders of index-linked government bonds, the Chancellor delayed the change until 2030 (see Reuters 2020b; FT 2020f). As the government itself explained 'the Chancellor has announced that while he sees the statistical arguments of UKSA's (UK Statistics Authority) intended approach to reform, *in order to minimise the impact of reform on the holders of index-linked gilts* he will be unable to offer his consent to the implementation of such a proposal before the maturity of the final specific index-linked gilt in 2030' (Reuters 2020a).

Inflation is a political issue, thus when UK policymakers choose to index it has implications not just for the Treasury, in terms of fiscal spending, but also for those that rely on these payments in everyday life. To come back to the argument of the book, the wealth of those at the top is impacted by indexing choices given the composition of their wealth, as outlined in Chapter 2. Here, choices to defer changes in indexing benefited those with assets in the form of bonds at the detriment of those whose pension comes from government transfers (state pension).

3.3 Covid Fortunes—Why Did the Economic Response Worsen Wealth Inequality

Having outlined Treasury and Bank of England measures we will close this chapter by showing some concrete examples of the effect of the pandemic upon the wealthiest. When examining those at the top of the income and wealth distribution in the UK, it is first worth noting the very extreme variations, or stratifications within this group. Danny Dorling described the UK's 1% as horizontally stratified from the high-income earners with salaries upwards of £150,000, taxed at the highest rate by the Treasury, to millionaires, and from there it is the asset-rich multi-million and billionaires who make up the 0.01%, the so-called high-net-worth individuals. As expected, globally the ultra-rich have done well in the pandemic. It has been reported that the world's five wealthiest individuals saw their collective worth increase by more than $250 billion (FT 2021a). The richest man in the world, Amazon founder Jeff Bezos, saw his wealth rise by an estimated $48 billion between March and June 2020. Elon Musk, the founder of Tesla motors, accrued an additional $17.2 billion over the same period. In the US alone, billionaires increased their total net worth by $637 billion during the pandemic (Business Insider 2020). Globally, Forbes estimated that the world's billionaire class was 20% richer by December 2020 (Reuters 2021) than before the pandemic.

Meanwhile the Knight Frank Wealth Report (2021: 16) predicts, based on recent trends, that the global population of ultra-high-net-worth individuals would grow by 27% over the next five years, while the number of high-net-worth individuals would rise by 41%. As such, the global shock vastly increased the fortunes of the ultra-rich. And indeed, each year since 2015 the Swiss Bank UBS has published a so-called 'Billionaires Report', noting that before the pandemic (between 2009 and 2020) the wealth of billionaires in the UK rose from $77bn to $205bn, an increase of 168% (UBS 2020: 22). Such runaway wealth at the top drives the ultra-wealthy even further away from the rest of society.

Focusing more specifically on those at the top of the UK wealth distribution they have gained most from financial investments, property, and private pensions (see Langley 2020: 388 for a summary). A Brown Shipley (2020) survey of 1100 wealthy individuals, confirmed that the performance of their pensions, their financial investments, and the property market were the three most important factors having helped them to amass financial assets.

Financial assets are almost entirely concentrated among the rich, which makes them a particularly important factor in the inequality discussion. After the 2008 financial crisis, the strong growth in financial assets 'caused wealth inequality to rise at a fast pace' (Credit Suisse 2021: 41). Between 2008 and 2020 financial assets rose from approximately 50.5% of gross assets to approximately 55.5% (ibid.). The same pattern emerged during the Covid-19 pandemic, with financial assets proving to be a major driver of wealth gains (Resolution Foundation 2021: 35). By August 2020, business as usual returned to global stock markets, with commentators declaring a rapid V-shaped recovery (*The Guardian* 2020a; UBS 2020: 6). By the end of 2021, the MSCI world index of developed market shares had risen by 22% between 2020 and 21 (MSCI 2022), signalling windfall gains for asset holders.

In fact, the economic woes affecting the UK economy at large appeared 'to have become completely detached from' wealth creation, where 'share price rises…benefited those in the upper wealth echelons' (Credit Suisse 2021: 25). In fact, the rise in financial asset prices (benefiting the rich), and the recovery of global financial markets, led many commentators to remark on the bizarre fact that while the UK economy was experiencing its worst performance since the great winter of 1709, stocks and bonds were booming. This should not come as such a surprise however, for those following the financialisation of multinational corporations and the ascent of the asset economy in the UK; a crisis facing the national economy has little impact on the capacity for making a profit (or profiteering).

Those at the top of the wealth distribution also benefitted via their ownership stakes in private pension funds. Again, as we noted with non-reforms of fiscal policy, it was not necessarily that public policy interventions added massive gains to the value of private pensions, but that interventions insulated these schemes from major losses. As markets crashed towards the end of February 2020, private pension schemes were particularly at risk. This is because those private pensions are heavily exposed to stock markets. In the UK, approximately 9.9 million people—among the richer households—now have private pensions; the number had increased almost tenfold since the 2008 financial crisis (*The Guardian* 2020c). By the end of the first quarter of 2020, the average private pension fund had fallen by 15%, the worst quarterly performance on record (FT 2020). BoE interventions were crucial to restoring the fortunes of these private pension funds by stabilising markets and restoring the prosperity of asset owners.

On average, pension funds lost approximately 15.2% between January and March 2020, but recovered approximately 13.3% in the second quarter (FT Adviser 2020). The majority of these gains were attributed to the recovery in financial markets enabled by central-bank monetary policy. In relation to wealth inequality, private pensions benefit from government subsidies, protections, and indexing practices which are deployed to support those in the higher tax bracket as we have already outlined above. Protecting private pension funds—assets of relevance to the rich—during the pandemic, using both monetary and fiscal policy measures further contributes to inequality.

The final major component of asset-based wealth in the UK among the rich is property ownership. Taking a bird's-eye view of 25 developed countries, the Economist magazine (2020) showed that real house prices rose by an average of 5% across the board during the pandemic. Those in Britain increased by 8% (ibid.). Moreover, the value of the UK's housing stock hit a new record high of £7.56 trillion, more than four times the value of all the companies in the FTSE100 (Savills 2021). The value of this housing stock rose £380 billion in 2020, making it the fastest annual increase since 2015. Of this, the north of England saw the strongest growth while London and the south-east accounted for 23% and 18% respectively of the total (ibid.). A more detailed discussion of house-price increases in the UK is covered in the next chapter, where housing is the main asset class of the middle-income group (Resolution Foundation 2021: 32). However, it is important to note that the wealthiest households also benefited from rising property prices due to the range of properties they possess. Property ownership can be of commercial real-estate, ownership of development companies (that hold real-estate portfolios), and as landlords of commercial or residential property. What distinguishes the wealthiest households from the rest, is the extent to which they hold property as a form of financial asset and how they can diversify within their property portfolio. This means that while rising property prices might make the biggest difference to the wealth of the middle-income households (in relative terms), in absolute terms the rich benefit the most (Resolution Foundation 2021: 34).

Setting aside the accumulation of wealth due to property ownership, the Covid-19 pandemic also showed how the quality of residential property is closely tied to health and well-being inequality as well. As such, there was considerable evidence of the mega-rich (0.1%) investing in UK country estates and high-end properties to allow for a more enjoyable lockdown experience (*The Guardian* 2020b). Media stories report multi-millionaires with £35 million mansions looking for separate four-bedroom duplex apartments costing £18,000 a month to rent, to self-isolate from other 'at risk' (vulnerable) family members (*Evening Standard* 2020). In other words, the pandemic showed (once again) that your home was far more than either simply a place to lay your head (for the poor) or an asset to supplement low savings and insufficient retirement funds (for the middle).

3.4   Closing Thoughts

This chapter argues that the UK's Covid-19 economic response supported the asset economy and lead to windfall gains at the top. Firstly, we addressed the central bank, which is responsible for interest rates, money, and market stability via monetary policy. We outlined how monetary measures boosted asset prices during the initial shock of the pandemic and how cautious the central bank is about winding down state support for asset markets. Secondly, the Treasury, which is responsible for taxation and expenditure via the budget and fiscal policy, made the decision to delay reform of capital gains tax as well as delayed implementation of indexing of private pensions. These are technocratic ways of supporting the wealthiest households during the pandemic.

UK policymakers were guided by an attempt to protect asset owners and, as such, the fault lines of inequality worsened. We argue, to prioritise asset-market stability over public services only serves to worsen overall economic stability. Such staggering interventions in financial markets were to protect the already rich from suffering hardship, while outright refusing to offer those already living in poverty additional protection as the pandemic unfolded.

References

Bank of England. 2020a. Bank of England Monetary Policy Report Press Conference, Thursday 5 November.

Bank of England. 2020b. Bank of England measures to respond to the economic shock from COVID19, 11 March.

Bank of England. 2020c. Asset Purchase Facility: Asset purchases and TFSME—Market Notice, 19 March.

Bank of England. 2020d. Remarks on COVID19 and Monetary Policy, Speech given by Professor Jonathan Haskel, External Member of the Monetary Policy Committee Brighton Chamber of Commerce, 1 July.

Bank of England. 2020e. The central bank balance sheet as a policy tool: Past, present and future, speech given by Andrew Bailey, 28 August, Jackson Hole Economic Policy Symposium.

Bank of England. 2020f. Monetary Policy Summary and minutes of the Monetary Policy Committee meeting ending on 4 August 2020.

Boyer, R. 2012. The four fallacies of contemporary austerity policies: The lost Keynesian legacy. *Cambridge Journal of Economics* 36 (1): 283–312.

Brown Shipley. 2020. Financial plans of the wealthy post-COVID19. Research Report. Available at https://brownshipley.com/en-gb/articles/fin ancial-plans-of-the-wealthy-post-covid-19. Accessed 17 November 2021.

Business Insider. 2020. How business insiders saw their net worth increase by half a trillion dollars during the pandemic, 30 October.

CityWire. 2020. Labour joins chorus calling for a wealth tax, 6 July.

Credit Suisse. 2021. Credit Suisse Wealth Report 2021.

Evening Standard. 2020. How coronavirus is affecting the super-rich: Billionaires search for country estates and islands to avoid COVID19, 19 March.

Financial Times. 2020a. How does QE help the coronavirus problem?, 27 March.

Financial Times. 2020b. BOE makes emergency rate cut to cushion economy, 11 March.

Financial Times. 2020c. Bank of England boosts bond-buying by £100bn but slows the pace, 18 June.

Financial Times. 2020d. Don't fight the Fed but don't depend on it either, 6 July.

Financial Times. 2020e. Andrew Bailey says BoE has ample 'firepower' to support UK economy, 28 August.

Financial Times. 2020f. UK to stop using RPI inflation measure in 2030, 25 November.

Financial Times. 2021a. COVID19: Widening the gap between rich and poor, 16 February.

Financial Times. 2021b. Budget will leave millions worse off next year, studies find, 28 October.

Financial Times Adviser. 2020. Pension see COVID recovery but annuities stay low, 4 August.

Financial Times Adviser. 2021. CGT gets another reprieve on 'tax day', 23 March.

FT. 2022. Prospering in the pandemic: The winners and losers of the Covid era, 3 January.

GMO. 2021. Waiting for the last dance: The hazards of asset allocation in at a late stage major bubble. Available at: https://www.gmo.com/europe/res earch-library/waiting-for-the-last-dance/. Accessed 11 January 2022.

Hedrick-Wong, Y. 2015. QE And Its Global Consequences. *Forbes*, 18 October.

Hope, D., and J. Limberg. 2022. The economic consequences of major tax cuts for the rich. Socio-Economic Review, mwab061. https://doi.org/10.1093/ser/mwab061.

Khan, O. 2020. *The Colour of Money: Race and economic inequality*. Runneymead Trust. Available at: https://www.runnymedetrust.org/blog/the-colour-of-money-race-and-economic-inequality. Accessed 31 January 2022.

Knight Frank. 2021. The Wealth Report. Available at: https://www.knightfrank.com/wealthreport. Accessed 20 January 2022.

Langley, P. 2020. Assets and assetization in financialized capitalism. *Review of International Political Economy* 28 (2): 382–393.

Montgomerie, J. 2016. Austerity and the household: The politics of economic storytelling. *British Politics* 11 (4): 418–437.

MSCI. 2022. MSCI World Index. Available at: https://www.msci.com/docume nts/10199/149ed7bc-316e-4b4c-8ea4-43fcb5bd6523. Accessed 11 January 2022.

OBR. 2021. October 2021 economic outlook. Available at: https://obr.uk/download/economic-and-fiscal-outlook-october-2021/. Accessed 11 January 2022.

Piketty, T. 2014. *Capital in the Twenty-First Century*, trans. A. Goldhammer. Cambridge, MA: Harvard University Press.

Resolution Foundation. 2020. Who Gains? The importance of accounting for capital gains, Resolution Foundation, May.

Resolution Foundation. 2021. (Wealth) Gap Year: The impact of the coronavirus crisis on UK household wealth, July.

Reuters. 2020a. Cresting "first wave" of stimulus may be next hurdle for world markets, 16 July.

Reuters. 2020b. UK delays change to RPI inflation in boost for bond buying investments, 25 November.

Reuters. 2021. In 2020 the ultra-rich got richer. Now they are bracing for the backlash, 25 March.

Reuters. 2022. Fed signals trigger world stocks, bonds sell off, 6 January.

Savills. 2021. UK housing value hits record £7.56 trillion high, 12 March.

Tax Justice UK. 2022. New figures show wealth and equality was entrenched before Covid, 7 January.

The Economist. 2020. House prices in the rich world are booming, 8 April.

The Guardian. 2020a. The only V shaped recovery after coronavirus will be in the stock markets, 18 August.

The Guardian. 2020b. Coronavirus: British pension set to take a hit from market tumbled, 29 February.

The Guardian. 2020c. From now, policies must put young people first. Starting with the triple lock pension, 19 June.

The Guardian. 2020d. Under cover of capital gains, the hyper rich have been getting richer than we thought, 21 May.

The Guardian. 2021a. Number of billionaires in UK reached new record during Covid crisis, 21 May.

The Guardian. 2021b. Treasury could raise £16 billion a year if shares and property were taxed like salaries, 26 October.

The Independent. 2021. UK billionaires see fortunes saw in pandemic, 21 May.

The Independent. 2022. Wealth of the richest one percent in UK more than 230 times that of the poorest 10%, ONS says, 9 January.

UBS. 2020. Riding the storm, Billionaires insights 2020. Available at: https://www.ubs.com/content/dam/static/noindex/wealth-management/ubs-billionaires-report-2020-spread.pdf. Accessed 19 November 2021.

University of Warwick. 2020. How much tax to the rich really pay you? New evidence from tax micro data in the UK. CAGE Policy Briefing Number 27, June.

Warren, T. 2006. Moving beyond the gender wealth gap: On gender, class, ethnicity, and wealth inequalities in the United Kingdom. *Feminist Economics* 12 (1–2): 195–219.

Whittaker, J. 2020. Modern Monetary Theory: The rise of economists who say huge government debt is not a problem. *The Conversation*, 7 July.

Wren-Lewis, S. 2014. Fiscal policy remains in the stone age. VoxEU, CEPR, 10 May 2018.

CHAPTER 4

A Squeezed Middle

Abstract The chapter looks at the effects of fiscal and monetary policy interventions and their impact on the middle—roughly 60% of the population. It argues that despite the scale of state intervention, notably the so-called furlough scheme and mortgage holidays, served to further squeeze the middle, who are less economically secure than before the pandemic. The UK's crisis response policies to insulate those in the middle followed the long-standing traditions of asset-based welfare where small-investment portfolios grow and residential house prices increase; however they provided *only* a sense of financial security for the middle, because incomes stagnate, debt levels increase, and financial insecurity festers. Using the household balance sheet to show the financial effect of government policies we develop an understanding of the deep fragilities of widening inequality that has built up over time. The final part of the chapter develops an understanding of the gendered and racialised dynamics of the inequalities in the 'middle' of the distribution. We argue that unequal outcomes are not down to skill or individual choice, but are firmly down to the structure of the economic system and policy choices.

Keywords Furlough · Mortgage holiday · Homeownership · Squeezed middle · Gender · Race

H. Macartney et al., *The Fault Lines of Inequality*, https://doi.org/10.1007/978-3-030-96914-1_4

4.1   Introduction

The term middle-class has different meanings in different countries, and in the UK, it refers to the affluent—those that have a sizable inheritance, are in a professional job, can send their kids to private school, and who can afford shopping at Waitrose weekly. Class is both material and cultural but is not simply a category of people 'in the middle' of the income distribution or working professional jobs. Here, we examine 'the middle' rather than the UK middle-class, which means we focus on the large grouping in the middle (four middle deciles, 5, 6, 7, 8) of the income and wealth distribution in the UK, covering approximately 60% of the population. This covers those who earn income from employment and have small financial holdings in residential housing and retail investments. This simple analytical frame does not capture the many different social groups that make up 'the middle' nor does it sufficiently address how gender and race differentiate within the middle strata of British society. Yet, we can show tendencies of experiences of the middle, compared to those at the top and the bottom.

Much has been made of the 'squeezed' middle in recent years. And indeed, this group has lost ground in economic terms, becoming increasingly fragile after the 2008 financial crisis. The middle has faced persistently stagnant incomes, when gains from employment do not grow in line with inflation there are small-scale wealth holdings, primary residences, and some with retail financial investments, such as pensions or stocks. This is in stark contrast to those at the top, who have enjoyed decades of real-terms (adjusted for inflation) income gains and skyrocketing increases in wealth from financial assets.

These conditions existed before the pandemic struck. Many policymakers believe that massive state intervention, like the Covid-19 response, would improve these conditions, or at the very least not make them worse by 'putting a floor under aggregate demand'. Our main argument in this chapter is that this is not the case. The UK's crisis response policies to insulate those in the middle follow the long-standing traditions of asset-based welfare where small-investment portfolios grow and residential house prices increase provided *only* a sense of financial security for the middle, because incomes stagnate, debt levels increase, and financial insecurity festers.

While many Covid-19 response measures may be novel, they still preserve and reinforce the asset economy's dynamics policymakers support—promoting asset ownership and homeownership as welfare for the middle as a form of 'privatised' Keynesian policy. Such welfare, while house prices are secure or even increasing, indeed gives a feeling of security for the moment, but what happens if this trend is reversed? Wealth is lost and financial insecurity compounded. The boom and bust of the credit-asset cycle, then leads to bailouts and austerity, further exacerbating inequality. Those in the middle have been impacted by over a decade of austerity as cuts to public services and transfers have permanently affected universal welfare. Echoing a culture of individual responsibility for one's own fortune and misfortune does not just affect the poor; it makes the middle more fragile. Therefore, the fault lines of inequality in the asset economy has the top pulling away, the middle squeezed under intense pressure, and an ever-larger chasm separating the bottom. What starts as economic inequality becomes deep division in society that fundamentally erodes cohesion and prosperity.

4.2   Covid-19 Intervention—The State's Role in Providing Social Security

Economic shocks are not rare, they typically start as a crisis in markets which is then transported into society. Covid-19 does not follow this pattern—the shock comes from a health threat in society bringing crisis into markets and as such does not conform to established routes of financial crisis as we have come to recognise them over the past 40 years. The impact of global health shock is most clearly seen in national economic measures of contraction in the immediate outbreak of Covid-19 in the UK. Our focus here is on government intervention, via public policy, to cope with the economic shockwave precipitated by the pandemic. Namely, for instance, in the crisis response policy measures adopted after the first national lockdown to protect from the economic shockwave.

For the middle, this has meant to break the connection between decreased economic activity (as measured by Gross Domestic Product) and unemployment or fall in income for the considerable number of people who rely on incomes from employment with the ability to sustain themselves, their household, and their community. Employment and unemployment figures offer a vantage point of the 'middle' which represents the largest segment of workers in the economy. 'The magnitude of the recession caused by the pandemic is unprecedented in modern times. GDP declined by 9.8% in 2020, the steepest drop since consistent records began in 1948 and the most in over three hundred years on some estimates' (Harari et al. 2021: 3). Such a sharp contraction, all at once and everywhere, is reflected in the impact on people's livelihoods which however is only partially captured in national statistics. For instance, the disruption to the routines of work and labour markets is observed in the early 2021 unemployment levels which increased 19%, up by 258,000 to 1.6 million; while employment levels reduced by 529,000, which was concentrated among young people (a fall of 310,000 employed 16–24 year olds) as they became economically inactive (Harari et al. 2021: 20). As of June 2021, the initial economic woes did not disappear, as attempts to find recovery in the number of payroll employees increased to 28.5 million (May 2021); still half a million (553,000) below pre-Covid levels, which is a substantial number of financially precarious households (Powell and Francis-Devine 2022). What this precariousness meant for households and the different members of these households cannot be seen by only looking at these data. Indeed, the scale of disruption to the patterns of work, leisure, care, and consumption caused by Covid-19 will have many unregistered or uncounted impacts that will only be known in time.

A key fiscal policy intervention was the Coronavirus Job Retention Scheme (CJRS, or furlough) which allowed employers to claim for 80% of salary for hours not worked to a maximum of £2,500 per month, explicitly targeting households at risk of income shock. Significantly, this model of 'employment insurance' was copied from other European nations (like Denmark, Germany, and the Netherlands) that have structured their welfare provision for the middle in this way at least since the financial crisis of 2007/8. While much was made of efforts to implement furlough, such a drastic measure was needed because the UK had no existing mechanism to support middle-income households. Furlough configured employment insurance to meet political commitments for only means-tested welfare, differing from the continental European schemes. Befitting the UK welfare state practice since the 1990s, furlough had strict eligibility criteria which targeted the 'salaried' worker in the middle of the distribution—£2,500 per month is exactly the 60th percentile of earnings in the UK labour market (ONS 2021). Undoubtedly furlough excluded high earners, but also large segments of non-salaried workers such as those working as contractors, flexible or temporary workers were excluded. The very workforce created by so-called 'active labour market' policies long championed by the Department of Work and Pension were not eligible for emergency income support during the global pandemic. While popular and much needed, the furlough scheme nevertheless was a measure which remained consistent with Conservative Party commitments to means-testing and time-limited welfare provision, this time for the salaried workers in the middle strata of society.

Since the UK government introduced the furlough scheme in March 2020, according to preliminary HMRC estimates after a year 11.2 million jobs were supported by the scheme by July 2021, totalling £53.8 billion in value of claims; as of 31 March 2021, approximately 14% of eligible jobs were still furloughed a year later, a total of 4.2 million jobs (Harari et al. 2021: 20). With the criteria for furlough support changing from July 2021 employers were required to contribute to the scheme with the scheme ending in September 2021. Time-limited benefits can only be a short-term fiscal response, which is a missed opportunity to further develop this policy into a mechanism for coping with the long-term impact of the Covid-19.

Besides furlough, there was a much smaller scale fiscal measure, the Self-Employed Income Support Scheme (SEISS), which targeted government income transfers to self-employed people to further cushion income shocks for small businesses. Applicants had to demonstrate how much their business turnover was impacted by the pandemic, a hurdle rate of 30% established to qualify. If business turnover was down less than 30% businesses were eligible for a £2,850 one-off grant, if turnover was down more than 30% businesses qualified for a £7,500 grant, all on the condition of re-opening the business and claiming the grant on annual business tax filing. The government reported uptake of the scheme, 'as of 31 January 2021, the SEISS has provided support to 2.7 million self-employed individuals, with claims totalling over £19.7 billion across the first three grants' (HM Treasury 2021: 11–12). Such comparatively tiny amounts of overall spending, mirrored in the paltry disbursement grants, are particularly stark when juxtaposed against the generous subsidies given to large multinational firms through both fiscal and monetary policies. Small businesses, which are overwhelmingly owned by those in the middle of the wealth and income distribution, were very much left to cope with the fallout of the pandemic without systemic or sustained long-term support from government.

Against this background, while much is made of the novelty of the UK's conservative government designing emergency measures and recovery package (*The Economist* 2021), there is a clear self-congratulatory ethos that doing something—anything—is better than doing nothing. The independent, but government-funded, Office for Budget Responsibility (OBR) narrates this framing of the pandemic response: '[outcomes would be much worse] without the measures the Government has taken. These have provided additional financial support to individuals and businesses through the lockdown. They should also help to limit any long-term economic "scarring", by keeping workers attached to firms and helping otherwise viable firms stay in business' (OBR 2020: 4). Here the temporal shift is important, without questioning if better policy today would lead to better social outcomes, instead there is a promise that whatever was done today has some unknown benefit (not 'scarring') in the future, just because it is done. Small business grants for the middle, while the rich receive zero-bound credit and central-bank bond-buying programmes, simply reproduce asset-based inequality trends present before the pandemic. Indeed, the fiscal response can be seen as even widening the chasms that divide the middle from the top and the bottom by making choices about where to intervene and with what types of policy measures.

Early reports from non-governmental organisations show the fault lines of inequality exist within the 'middle'—these fissures have remained constant during the pandemic. The UK's crisis response did not act to ameliorate the harm caused to those already facing discrimination and disadvantage, indeed, it made these groups within 'the middle' worse-off. When we look at the middle along gender lines, more women than men have been furloughed, more have taken on a greater share of caring responsibilities, and more have reported higher anxiety, depression, and loneliness. Gender inequality cascades through other social stratifications. In the UK, disabled women, women on low incomes, young women, and single women report lower levels of well-being and, along with Black, Asian, and ethnic minority women, lower levels of financial stability (Women's Budget Group et al. 2021: 3). These social stratifications also configure the middle of UK society, and the widening fault lines within the middle were similarly exacerbated by the government response.

The pandemic also made visible the clear tension within the middle to reproduce itself, as existing age-based inequalities within the UK is a sore spot. There are clear generational divides, which map voting preferences, in terms of the quality and protections afforded in the welfare and employment systems which disproportionately disadvantage younger generations. When Covid-19 hit, the younger generation were again uniquely disadvantaged compared to other age cohorts within the 'middle'. '[T]he labour market shocks associated with the coronavirus (Covid-19) pandemic have been felt more by young people and the lowest paid; people aged under 30 years and those with household incomes under £10,000 were around 35% and 60%, respectively, more likely to be furloughed than the general population' (Benyon and Vassilev 2021). In other words, if pandemic response measures had been truly exceptional or different, then fiscal policy would have produced generalised welfare instead of intensifying inequality.

To summarise, the UK's economic response was successful in putting a floor under the incomes of the middle during the initial phase of the pandemic. Primarily via the furlough programme, which segmented relief to salaried workers, and much less so to small-business owners, whether trades people or consultants. Means-testing gave power to policymakers to decide who gets support during a global health crisis and who does not. Income levels overall were stabilised during a period of intense economic contraction; in simple terms this is a success. However, these temporary measures also served to further fracture existing fault lines of inequality.

As income inequality is unfortunately not about aspiration or individual choice, the segmented structure of labour markets creates income stratification. If you are a salaried worker, or a contractor, this structure matters as much as your skill level in determining your level of financial security. Welfare then is a form of social security, no matter whether it is accessed as a 'tax break' (stamp duty relief) or 'income transfer' (furlough, universal credit), or as services (NHS). By targeting state relief measures at specific segments of the employment market the outcome is greater income inequality between different strata of society.

Means-testing emergency welfare measures is not exceptional, it is consistent with the political agenda that created inequality as a societal problem in the first place. CJRS and SEISS show the dual paths of support, which only further worsened the gulfs between incomes in the segmented labour market. The pandemic needed universal measures to put a firm floor under all incomes and got the opposite. In part, this is how the UK's Covid response only further contributed to the unequal gender, racial, age-based, and location-based outcomes. An established economic policy agenda already determined who was protected (asset holders) and who was made worse-off (everyone else) by the pandemic recovery policy agenda. Universal welfare provision on the other hand would stabilise the polarisation between the top, the middle, and the bottom—ensuring inequality does not worsen during the global health crisis.

4.3   Housing-Based Welfare Works as Designed

Alongside temporary fiscal measures, the UK's economic policy response used the asset-based welfare measures, via monetary policy targeting residential housing, to stabilise the 'middle' sentiments and confidence. For decades, residential homeownership has been promoted as a form of 'privatised' welfare (or privatised Keynesianism) in which owner-occupiers rely on low-interest rates and rising property values to access debt that drives consumption, which becomes national aggregate growth. Large-scale measures like the BoE's monetary policy targeting of mortgage lending is sending a clear signal to banks to lend to the residential housing market. Taxation policy, via Treasury's Stamp Duty relief, sent a clear stimulating signal to residential housing markets. Further government support was committed to tie the construction and property development industry to recover plans: the Spending Review committed a £7.1 billion National Home Building Fund, a subsidy of £100 million to the 'brownfield land and support innovative construction techniques' as well as a £2.2 billion 'Help to Build' equity loan scheme.

Even before Covid-19 economic policy measures were linked to increases in housing prices, which became an important policy lever used during the pandemic. Indeed, the continuity of privatised Keynesianism is best illustrated in policy efforts to galvanise credit-driven house-price increases. Housing-based welfare works because it facilitates a sense of financial gains for all existing homeowners, rising house values give a sense of wealth increasing without having to sell and find other suitable housing. Significantly though, homeownership is an important axis of wealth inequality in which large groups in society, even those with high incomes are 'locked out' (Adkins et al. 2020) from homeownership because of rising prices.

During a pandemic, while people are told to 'stay-at-home' the government economic response sought to give those 'owner-occupiers' and private property owners that own homes as 'assets' a boost by driving up asset values. From June 2020 to May 2021, the average price of a UK home rose 13.4%, which was reported in The Guardian as 'the highest annual growth rate since November 2004' the same level as at the height of market euphoria before the reality of the 2008 crash (Kollewe 2021). The Bank of England's outgoing chief economist, Andy Haldane, recently said the [housing] market was 'on fire' and that the dramatic price gains were highly likely to worsen inequality between the better-off, many of whom have accumulated savings during the pandemic, and younger people (Kollewe 2021). In effect, financialisation and housing-based welfare connects owner-occupiers, private renters, and private landlords in the provision of shelter for society.

Importantly, the UK's housing-based welfare regime leads to geographically uneven and intergenerationally unequal wealth gains. Inasmuch as residential property market values and turnover are highly dependent on the region, proximity to an urban centre, and can be highly variable down to the level of the postal code (Montgomerie and Budenbender 2015). Reaching record house-price gains during the pandemic can easily be misunderstood as providing a generalised gain, in which house prices going up is a good enjoyed by everyone. For instance, Northern Ireland and Wales experiencing the largest year-on-year increases of 14% and 13.1%, respectively, is different from putting a floor under incomes; it means housing in these areas becomes more unaffordable for non-homeowners.

Pumping up house prices only benefited some segments in society and concentrated wealth gains in urban centres further exacerbating age-based and regional inequalities in the UK. London's residential property market is among the most expensive in the world, and a 7.3% increase in prices with this global city in 'lockdown', represents substantial gains in the fictional or notional value of property. While a similar 7.1% increase in Scotland gives a boost to existing homeowners, but represents smaller gains in value terms, yet only further prices out those excluded by price from owning a home. For example, in June 2021 the average annual price increase for a first-time buyer was 12.7% (Money Charity 2021), general price increases elsewhere lead to further unaffordability, which worsens wealth inequality. The UK's Covid-19 economic crisis response activated housing-based welfare to provide a privatised safety net. Asset-based welfare excludes non-asset owners, which in the case of housing is those groups in society that do not have enough deposit (the young, those without family wealth) or do not qualify for enough mortgage borrowing (those on middle and low incomes). The state trying to increase house prices with monetary policy only benefit existing owner-occupiers and private landlords, thus widening wealth inequality and social security of those not already in the residential housing market. Thus, using housing-based welfare as a mechanism for delivering Covid-19 economic relief only added to the differences in relief experienced by different stratifications of society and further widened already existing gaps.

4.4   DEBT AND SAVING

To understand how fiscal and monetary policies impact the middle requires us to connect these 'macro' policies to the 'micro' level of everyday life. However, rather than take the individual, we examine the household—more specifically the household balance sheet as a straightforward way of analysing the financial effect of government policies on those in the middle. This is because the degree to which residential housing acts as a privatised Keynesian safety net is established (Montgomerie 2016; Sparkes and Wood 2021). Thus, we look at the stylised frame of the *balance sheet* of the middle, which looks at the aggregate level, but which hides a deep fragility built up over a long-time widening inequality, which only mildly changes the arithmetic mean of aggregate measures. A protracted economic shock however, like the current pandemic, poses an ongoing threat to income sources for those in the middle, so that the financial stability remains fragile even if asset values increase. To exemplify; a recent study of the employment effects of the pandemic ran along the established market segments: 'Of those who have not been able to work (either because of being on furlough or for another reason), over half (52%) of people in the top income quintile continued to be paid in full, while this was the case for only 28% of those in the lowest income quintile' (Benyon and Vassilev 2021). The middle sits between these two poles with its own unevenness and segmentations, which are deeply connected to how housing is used as a form of privatised welfare.

Often these dynamics appear as intergenerational inequality, or the differences between different age cohorts rather than stratifications between top, middle, and bottom. This dynamic is highlighted in the Benyon and Vassilev (2021) report in these terms: 'People with a job or seeking work were more likely to have decreased income during the pandemic, and particularly the poorest 20%, while others such as retired people out of the labour market were more protected' (p. 12). While intergenerational inequality certainly overlaps with other stratifications, it would be problematic to reduce one to the other. And indeed, a global health crisis exposed the ways in which health and social welfare are provided in the UK, and its distinctly financialised characteristic is why inequality got worse on different stratifications, not just stayed the same, as a result of the pandemic.

Considering residential housing, as the main financial asset of those in the middle, mainly as owner-occupiers but including as small private landlords, we can see how asset-based welfare protects the balance sheet of those at the middle while not supporting income or consumption to the same degree. In effect, house-price increases are being used to support the notional value of the household balance sheet, giving a psychological uplift rather than income support. We see this already in the increase of household debt-to-income ratios (DTI compares how much is owed each month to how much is earned before taxes) before the pandemic. This ratio was at 127% in March 2020, increasing to 130% in March 2021 (ONS 2021). This aggregate creeping up of the amount of debt owed compared to income earned, is unevenly distributed across society, even among groups in the middle of the distribution. During the pandemic, the national household debt stock reached £1.7 trillion, which means of those households with debt their holdings increased by £67.3 billion over the 12 months June 2020–21, equivalent to an extra £1,273 of borrowing per UK adult (Money Charity 2021).

Of course, not everyone had to borrow. Rather, the additional £67 billion of new debt during the pandemic were taken on by groups in society. How this new debt burden is distributed, via residential mortgages and consumer credit products, is at the centre of how debt is used as a safety net. Emergency measures to provide 'debt holidays' for borrowers on mortgages and consumer credit products were activated as part of forbearance measures. Payment Deferral Guidance (PDG) did not include automatic stops on interest accrual, although some firms introduced this (Financial Conduct Authority 2021a). Granting only six months of mortgage holidays (from May to October 2020) was a minimalist measure, but demonstrates a unique protection afforded to homeowners and debtors in the middle. Debt guidance was issued in January 2021 regarding mortgages and instructed debt collection agencies and banks not to enforce repossessions before April 2021, however repossessions of goods and vehicles were permitted from 31 January 2021. The FCA noted that: 'Our approach reflects the different risks and harms that customers with goods or vehicles on credit are likely to face compared to those who are at risk of losing their home at this time' (Financial Conduct Authority

2021b). This echoed Chancellor Sunak's statement at the beginning of the crisis in which he described government intervention as necessary to '…keep a roof over your head' (HM Treasury and Sunak MP 2020).

Looking closer at the lending practices, the Financial Lives Survey for 2021, reported that since March 2020, there had been around 4.5 million payment deferrals (across mortgages and consumer credit products) with high-cost credit firms less likely to have the range of crisis mitigation measures in place than other types of credit firms (Financial Conduct Authority 2021a). Furthermore, women were more likely to be classed as financially vulnerable than men and while men are slightly more likely than women to hold credit products, 13% of women and 8% of men were found to hold or have held a high-cost credit product in the last twelve months (Financial Conduct Authority 2021b). Thus, inequality in this context is what separates why, on the one hand, some households have no need to borrow and, on the other hand, some rely on debt to meet the basic means of survival.

This gulf between those households that borrow out of necessity and those out of choice is significant. The 2020 Financial Lives survey showed that, pre-crisis, 85% of adults had held or were holding at least one credit or loan product in the last year and that this was an increase of 78% since the 2017 survey (Financial Conduct Authority 2021b). As noted, the BoE recognised early in the pandemic that demand from households for short-term credit would be enhanced by the crisis (Bank of England 2020a). However, the House of Commons report showed that, on the aggregate, households reduced their spending, increased their savings, and paid down their debts, suggesting a stable household sector (Francis-Devine 2021).

Taking a distributional approach contrasts the good news of increasing aggregate household savings and debt remaining at a consistent level with the evidence suggesting some households, particularly those with lower incomes, have run down savings and increased debt since the start of the pandemic. The Office for National Statistics found that by December 2020, nearly 9 million people had to borrow more money than usual because of coronavirus. Closer consideration of the figures reveals that lower income households are more likely to have increased their debt levels and decreased savings and that this increased debt is being used to meet the cost of essentials such as food and housing (Francis-Devine 2021) (see also Chapter 5). Here a new fault line is appearing dividing the middle-income groups among those with and without consumer debt.

When talking about debt we also need to talk about saving and there is growing recognition by the Bank of England, based on internal research, suggesting households that have increased their savings will be more reluctant to spend, widening the gulf between those that did not suffer income or wealth shocks and those that did (Bank of England 2020b). This is a risky strategy for economic rebuilding. In part making people spend was the justification for state subsidies to the hospitality industry in the creation of the 'Eat Out to Help Out' scheme, which provided government reimbursement to hospitality establishments for 50% of food bills from Monday to Wednesday through August 2020. The Treasury described this policy as '…keeping more money in hardworking families' pockets and giving a vital boost to the UK's hospitality sector' (HM Treasury 2020). Indeed, this scheme sought to incentivise households to resume consumption of food outside the home using their accumulated savings, the goal was to stimulate what the Treasury believed would be low demand during the pandemic (Hutton, 2020). Similarly, lockdown scepticism relies heavily on the notion that keeping the economy going with consumer spending is legitimising the acceptance of higher coronavirus figures. All this relies on the idea that consumer spending is increasing when allowed to happen.

Here, the welfare function of the state is hugely distorted as it seeks to tie together what it sees as aggregate savings to revive the economy (with the hospitality industry having suffered a 90% fall in economic output during the first phase of lockdown) (Hutton and Foley 2021). The belief that the middle could drive a recovery by consuming demonstrates a clear bias towards those that did not suffer an income shock as targets of intervention, believing spending would trickle down to those left unemployed due to the pandemic. At a time when food poverty and food bank use was skyrocketing even among the lower income groups in the middle, additional support to get the middle spending again only reproduced the established fault lines of income inequality in the UK.

We have already traced the asset economy back to the liberalisation of financial markets in the 1980s when wealth inequality began to worsen. We have outlined how the 'unacknowledged' privatised Keynesian policy regime relies on credit-fuelled asset growth to drive wealth and debt-driven consumption to drive demand (Crouch 2009). This blueprint is prominent in the UK, and part of a wider spread Anglo-American 'asset economy'. Again, as outlined by Adkins et al. (2020) the asset, rather than commodity, is generating logics that integrate global financial markets into everyday life. Here, the key element shaping inequality is not only the employment relationship, but also the capacity to buy assets that appreciate at a faster rate than both inflation (how much all prices go up) and wages (income from employment). Employment remains a key factor as it shapes the ability to purchase assets—stocks or to secure a mortgage to buy a house—but this is one among other significant wealth generating factors like family wealth transfer and inheritance, age, gender, race, and where you live.

4.5   Inclusion in the Squeezed Middle—Gender and Racial Inequality

The remainder of this chapter examines how the pandemic response has compounded inequalities within the 'middle' of the distribution, specifically the gender and racial dynamics of economic inequality. In the UK, gender and racial dimensions overlap with attainment of status within the 'large middle' of the income and wealth distribution scale. Gender and racial inequality can be seen in economic terms, like pay gaps and wealth gaps (Khan 2020; Kabeer et al. 2021). Financial Conduct Authorities' 'Financial Lives Survey 2020' (2021a) reported that there had been a disproportionate impact of the pandemic on the financial lives of younger and ethnic minority households (Financial Conduct Authority 2021b). The significance of gender and race to inequality in society is however much broader than purely economic, because social hierarchies encompass a range of economic and social relationships including unpaid caring work in the home or forms of systemic discrimination.

Focusing on the asset economy opens new avenues for considering the structural and political importance of 'the middle' in the UK's financialised economy. In gendered and racialised terms, having access to and representation in the middle strata of society is the product of generations of struggle for equality. Access to stable employment, public services, housing, and high levels of consumption remain the middle-class dream of being 'upwardly mobile' on the income ladder. Yet access to asset gains from portfolio investments and residential housing are small-scale; and impossible without the ongoing public subsidy of low-interest rates and housing-based welfare. These trajectories up and down the income ladder are also between social strata, and these relationships are deeply gendered and racialised in UK society. Women and minorities, overall, earn less and hold less wealth, especially housing wealth (Warren 2006; Francis-Devine

2021). Importantly, this means that unequal economic outcomes are not down to skills or individual choice, they are firmly down to the structure of the economic system.

Recognising gender and racial dynamics of those in 'the middle' of the asset economy provides a necessary recognition of the encoded social logic that permit stratifications in the first place. Therefore, when interpreting the UK's pandemic economic response special attention was paid to identifying the asset logics of the privatised Keynesian paradigm, and further considering how the gender and racial dynamics play out.

It is understood that the Covid-19 public health response required a cessation of a considerable proportion of economic activity, which did not have a uniform effect. Moving a sizeable portion of economic activity into the household, or domestic sphere, via stay-at-home orders, lockdowns, and school closures, had profoundly gendered and racialised effects. Lockdowns put strain on the domestic home, where the burden of unpaid work disproportionately falls to women. The need to care for, and provide education for children, in the household, highlighted the problems this gendered division of labour creates for the wider economy but is most acute in the middle of the distribution. A key component of women's gains in the labour market is predicated on access to childcare, but as cultural norms of gender equality reach into the home, childcare also benefits men with childcare responsibilities. The Women's Budget Group (2020) found that the gendered differences in the burden of childcare were enhanced, not reduced, by the pandemic, there was no renegotiation of the caring burden. Mothers were likely to have worked less, and had their work interrupted more because their children were at home, than fathers (Women's Budget Group et al. 2020). The need to care affects all parents and will have long-term impacts, particularly for single parents, the majority of whom are mothers, and those in lower-paid and insecure work. Partly as a result of the loss of employment, all parents in an IFS survey were found to be doing less paid work and more childcare in response to the Covid-19 crisis (Andrew et al. 2020), with women still being disproportionally affected. Throughout the pandemic response it was clear policymakers routinely failed to recognise the role that childcare plays in supporting access to well-paid work.

And indeed, while all parents have been affected by the need to carry out more childcare, the provision of childcare is and remains gendered in the UK. How childcare is provided has important implications for access to paid employment, thus the gendered nature of childcare will reflect in paid employment. For example, formal childcare provision operates around standard working hours, 9am–6pm, Monday to Friday. Employment, particularly in highly gendered sectors impacted by the pandemic including health and social care, is a 24 hour role. Many workers in these sectors rely on the care provided by grandparents because it is cheap and flexible (Women's Budget Group et al. 2021). When the pandemic hit and grandparents had to be excluded from childcare routines, those that most heavily relied on these childcare arrangements were necessarily most affected and it became impossible for many to hold on to their jobs. And indeed, more women than men lost their job during the Covid-19 economic crisis; also, women were more likely than men to have been furloughed (Women's Budget Group 2021). While parents are entitled to ask for furlough because of childcare needs the Trade Unions Congress found that 71% of women who applied during the last school lockdown were refused (Trades Union Congress 2021). These outcomes further suggest the gendered divisions in employment markets were only exacerbated by the economic fallout of the Covid-19 pandemic.

The Chair of the Women and Equalities Committee, Caroline Nokes MP, referred to the ways in which policies exacerbated social inequalities as 'institutional thoughtlessness' (Nokes 2021). Choices regarding inclusion or exclusion of certain information, and in particular the way this replication of gender exclusionary practices happens through informal institutions, uncodified rules that by their nature are not always perceivable (Waylen 2017) is demonstrative of the gendered nature of institutions. The agents of these structures refuse to 'see' the evidence of the problem, because it is not in their interests and the institutions are reinforced as a result.

Scientific data on the spread of Covid-19 clearly mapped on to existing health inequalities of ethnic minority groups in the UK (Public Health England 2020) who are disproportionally affected by deprivation, and we will return to this in the following chapter (see: Nazroo 2003). Yet, Covid-19 and the policy response further worsened racial inequality not just in health terms but also in wealth and income terms, because of existing labour and financial market segmentation which is a structural cause of unequal outcomes. Byrne et al., (2020) up-to-date snapshot of the racial segmentation of UK labour markets shows that individuals from ethnic minority backgrounds face several powerful external drivers that have changed, and continue to change, the nature of work and labour markets to disadvantage them relative to the majority white-British workforce (127–28).

A recent national survey on the impact of Covid-19 by Runnymede Trust (Haque et al. 2021) showed that pre-existing racial and socioeconomic inequalities have not only been amplified by the coronavirus crisis: they have been made worse. The survey revealed that some ethnic minority groups—such as Bangladeshi and Black African groups—have experienced significant income loss during the coronavirus crisis, and two-thirds of members of ethnic minority groups (65%, compared with 46% of people in white groups) have struggled with paying bills and paying for essentials during lockdown. Ethnic minority groups have also been less likely to receive any form of sick pay if ill with the coronavirus, even though they have had to self-isolate. Seeing policy interventions through the lens of existing structural inequalities goes some way to explaining why despite large-scale fiscal and monetary interventions those in the middle did not do better, indeed suggesting why there are clear gender and racial disparities in health and wealth outcomes. 'Doing something' was depicted by state policymakers as better than 'doing nothing' in response to the shock of the pandemic. However, this chapter highlights that—in wealth, race, and gender dimensions—the middle, who were aided by the government support measures, have suffered nonetheless as social and economic divides worsened.

4.6   Closing Thoughts

This chapter further connected the long-established practice of privatised Keynesianism and housing-based welfare with the present-day asset economy and its impact on the middle of Britain's wealth and income strata. We demonstrated how the UK government's economic response sought to promote housing-price increases to give the perception of a stable balance sheet, as asset values increased but debt obligations remained the same (or deferred by up to six months), while the threats to the budget sheet of those in the middle, reductions in income levels and rising expenditure, remain a persistent feature of the pandemic. Housing-based welfare cannot deliver generalised welfare gains, it gives more gains to existing homeowners, while excluding everyone else.

Importantly inequality in the asset economy is not strictly an economic problem. Inequality breeds division in society, what drives the poles apart is a deep friction that is not easy to contain. The chapter closed by highlighting a variety of the racial and gendered dimensions of inequality affected by the government's coronavirus response measures.

REFERENCES

Adkins, L., M. Cooper, and M. Konings. 2020. *The asset economy*. Wiley.

Andrew, A., S. Cattan, M.C. Dias, et al. 2020. How are mothers and fathers balancing work and family under lockdown? *Institute for Fiscal Studies*. Available at: https://www.ifs.org.uk/publications/14860.

Bank of England. 2020a. Quantitative easing—Fact sheet, gov.co.uk, November. Available at: https://www.bankofengland.co.uk/monetary-policy/quantitative-easing. Accessed 12 November 2021.

Bank of England. 2020b. Bank of England Monetary Policy Report Press Conference, Thursday 5 November.

Benyon and Vassilev. 2021. Personal and economic wellbeing estimates by those with and without a disability, across time. Office for National Statistics.

Byrne, B., C. Alexander, and W. Shankley. 2020. *Ethnicity, race and inequality in the UK: State of the nation*. Policy Press.

Crouch, C. 2009. Privatised Keynesianism: An unacknowledged policy regime. *BJPIR* 11: 382–399.

Financial Conduct Authority. 2021a. Financial Lives 2020 survey: The impact of coronavirus, 11 February. Available at: https://www.fca.org.uk/publication/research/financial-lives-survey-2020.pdf. Accessed 26 April 2021.

Financial Conduct Authority. 2021b. Financial Conduct Authority. 2020a. Coronavirus: information for consumers with personal loans, overdrafts and other forms of credit. Available at: https://www.fca.org.uk/consumers/coronavirus-information-personal-loans-credit-cards-overdrafts. Accessed 30 April 2021.

Francis-Devine, B. 2021. Coronavirus: Impact on household debt and savings. House of Commons Library. Available at: https://researchbriefings.files.parliament.uk/documents/CBP-9060/CBP-9060.pdf. Accessed 28 April 2021.

Harari, D., M. Keep, and P. Brien. 2021. *Coronavirus: Economic Impact*. London: House of Commons. Available at: https://researchbriefings.files.parliament.uk/documents/CBP-8866/CBP-8866.pdf. Accessed 13 January 2021.

Haque, Z., L. Becares, and N. Treloar. 2021. *Over-exposed and under-protected* (p. 24) [Research Report]. Runnymede Trust.

HM Treasury. 2020. Eat Out to Help Out launches today - with government paying half on restaurant bills, 3 August. Available at: https://www.gov.uk/government/news/eat-out-to-help-out-launches-today-with-government-paying-half-on-restaurant-bills. Accessed 19 May 2021.

HM Treasury. 2021. Budget Speech 2021. Available at: https://www.gov.uk/government/speeches/budget-speech-2021. Accessed 15 April 2021.

HM Treasury and Sunak MP, T.R.H.R. 2020. A Plan for Jobs speech, 8 July. Available at: https://www.gov.uk/government/speeches/a-plan-for-jobs-speech. Accessed 2 May 2021.

Hutton, G. 2020. Eat Out to Help Out Scheme. House of Commons Library. Available at: https://commonslibrary.parliament.uk/research-briefings/cbp-8978/. Accessed 19 May 2021.

Hutton, G., and N. Foley. 2021. *Hospitality Industry and Covid-19, CBP 91.* London: House of Commons Library. Available at: https://commonslibrary.parliament.uk/research-briefings/cbp-9111/. Accessed 19 May 2021.

Kabeer, N., S. Razavi, and Y. van der Meulen Rodgers. 2021. Feminist economic perspectives on the COVID-19 pandemic. *Feminist Economics* 27 (1–2): 1–29. https://doi.org/10.1080/13545701.2021.1876906.

Khan, O. 2020. *The Colour of Money: Race and economic inequality.* Runneymead Trust. Available at: https://www.runnymedetrust.org/blog/the-colour-of-money-race-and-economic-inequality. Accessed 31 January 2022.

Kollewe, J. 2021. UK house prices rise at fastest rate since 2004 amid stamp duty rush, 29 June.

Money Charity. 2021. United Kingdom Monthly Money Statistics Report. Available at: Statistics Archive | The Money Charity. Accessed 13 January 2022.

Montgomerie, J. 2016. Austerity and the household: The politics of economic storytelling. *British Politics* 11 (4): 418–437.

Montgomerie, J., and M. Büdenbender. 2015. Round the houses: Homeownership and failures of asset-based welfare in the United Kingdom. *New Political Economy* 20 (3): 386–405. https://doi.org/10.1080/13563467.2014.951429.

Nazroo, J.Y. 2003. The structuring of ethnic inequalities in health: Economic position, racial discrimination, and racism. *American Journal of Public Health* 93 (2): 277–284. American Public Health Association. https://doi.org/10.2105/AJPH.93.2.277.

Nokes, C. 2021. The gendered economic impact of Covid-19. *BBC Radio 4 - Woman's Hour.* London. Available at: https://www.bbc.co.uk/programmes/m000s186. Accessed 16 March 2022.

The Economist. 2021. Boris Johnson's Conservatives plan to create a bigger, busier state, 11 March. Available at: https://www.economist.com/britain/2021/11/06/boris-johnsons-conservatives-plan-to-create-a-bigger-busier-state. Accessed 12 November 2021.

OBR. 2020. Coronavirus analysis. Available at: https://obr.uk/coronavirus-analysis/. Accessed 20 January 2022.

ONS. 2021. Personal and economic well-being in Great Britain: January 2021. Available at: https://www.ons.gov.uk/peoplepopulationandcommunity/wellbeing/bulletins/personalandeconomicwellbeingintheuk/january2021#savings-borrowing-and-affordability. Accessed 14 December 2021.

Powell, A., and B. Francis-Devine. 2022. Coronavirus: Impact on the labour market. Available at: https://commonslibrary.parliament.uk/research-briefings/cbp-8898/. Accessed 16 March 2022.

Public Health England. 2020. Disparities in the risk and outcomes of COVID-19. *Association of Medical Research Charities*. https://assets.publishing.service.gov.uk/government/uploads/system/uploads/attachment_data/file/908434/Disparities_in_the_risk_and_outcomes_of_COVID_August_2020_update.pdf.

Sparkes, M., and J.D.G. Wood. 2021. The political economy of household debt & The Keynesian policy paradigm. *New Political Economy* 26 (4): 598–615. Routledge. https://doi.org/10.1080/13563467.2020.1782364.

Trades Union Congress. 2020/2021. TUC poll: 7 in 10 requests for furlough turned down for working mums. News Listing, Organisation, 14 January. Available at: https://www.tuc.org.uk/news/tuc-poll-7-10-requests-furlough-turned-down-working-mums. Accessed 28 April 2121.

Warren, T. 2006. Moving beyond the gender wealth gap: On gender, class, ethnicity, and wealth inequalities in the United Kingdom. *Feminist Economics* 12 (1–2): 195–219.

Waylen, G. 2017. Gendering institutional change. In *The Oxford handbook of gender and politics*, ed. K. Celis, J. Kantola, S.L. Weldon, and G. Wyalen. First issued as an Oxford University Press paperback. Oxford: Oxford University Press. Available at: https://doi.org/10.1093/acrefore/9780190228637.013.237.

Women's Budget Group. 2020. Submission to the Women and Equalities Select Committee inquiry: Unequal impact? Coronavirus and the gendered economic impact, June. Available at: https://wbg.org.uk/wp-content/uploads/2020/06/WBG-Gender-economic-impact-submission.pdf. Accessed 9 April 2021.

Women's Budget Group. 2021. Social Care, Gender and Covid-19. Available at: https://wbg.org.uk/wp-content/uploads/2021/03/Social-care-gender-and-Covid-19.pdf. Accessed 26 April 2021.

Women's Budget Group, Close the Gap, Engender, Fawcett Society, Northern Ireland Women's Budget Group and Women's Equality Network Wales. 2021. One year on: Women are less likely than men to feel the Government's response to Covid-19 has met their needs, March. Available at: https://wbg.org.uk/analysis/reports/one-year-on-women-are-less-likely-than-men-to-feel-the-governments-response-to-covid-19-has-met-their-needs/. Accessed 12 April 2021.

CHAPTER 5

Precarity for Those at the Bottom

Abstract This chapter develops an understanding of what the asset economy and privatised Keynesianism mean for those who don't own assets. The shift from welfare provisions to asset-based welfare and individualised responsibility has resulted in a bare minimum financial support for those asset poor, accompanied by a narrative of personal responsibility for poverty, that was even kept alive during a once-in-a-lifetime pandemic. We develop an understanding of the time-limited and means-tested support for the poor as part of the Covid-19 response package and sketch key stylised examples of where economic and social policy overlap and connect to everyday life. We look at homelessness, food poverty, and child poverty to highlight the plight of the substantial group in society that has been left further behind as a result of economic policy choices during the pandemic. Furthermore, the chapter stresses the intersectionalities of inequality where, for example, race, age, gender, and nationality crucially co-determine the ability of people to own assets and thus to benefit from asset-based welfare.

Keywords Food poverty · Homelessness · Child poverty · Asset Poor · Debt

H. Macartney et al., *The Fault Lines of Inequality*,
https://doi.org/10.1007/978-3-030-96914-1_5

5.1   Introduction

As we have established, the Covid-19 pandemic has not had an equal effect on everyone. Indeed, while the political messaging of 'togetherness' littered commentaries throughout the crisis—'We can beat this virus together—but only if we stay alert', 'We are in this together and together we will prevail' (Boris Johnson on Facebook 17 May 2020), 'We will get through this winter together' (Boris Johnson, House of Commons Statement 22 September 2020), 'Together we can make this the peak' (Matt Hancock on BBC Breakfast 13 January 2021) or 'We are all on the same team in the battle against coronavirus and we will get through this together' (Matt Hancock, BBC daily coronavirus address 19 April 2020)—the experiences of the poor and asset-less, paints a very different picture of neglect.

In the first two chapters we outlined the fault lines of inequality at the heart of the UK. The asset economy is supported by privatised Keynesianism, which informs political decisions about resource allocation in crisis times. We have seen how those with assets benefit from various fiscal and monetary policies that create a safety net for asset values. A wider shift from government welfare provisions to asset-based welfare and individualised responsibility equates to provision of the absolute bare minimum financial support for those without assets by the state, accompanied by a harsh narrative emphasising personal responsibility. Even during a once-in-a-century pandemic, the narrative remains that it was the individual, more than anything else, who needs to 'work its way out of poverty' and take responsibility for misfortune.

If you pause to contemplate the implications of this asset-based welfare policy regime for those without assets it is both staggering and inhumane. What it says about the moral economy of the asset economy is indefensible and is why political change and government policies need to be introduced to remedy these ills.

Deploying a privatised Keynesian crisis response meant that fiscal spending to those at the bottom consisted of a minimal and temporary uplift. At the same time, these temporary measures, such as the evictions ban and the universal credit uplift, did little to ameliorate the worst effects of the crisis for the lowest income and least wealthy households. This is because, by the time the pandemic hit, decades of privatised Keynesianism had left the welfare state in ruins. In relation to our fault lines of inequality, Covid-19 therefore meant that those 'misfortunate' enough to find themselves at the bottom rungs of the economic ladder, did not qualify for the massive central-bank bailouts for those at the top, nor did they benefit from the fiscal floor put under the feet of the middle. Having already endured a decade of austerity prior to the pandemic (2010–2020) those at the bottom of the economic hierarchy had already experienced wholesale retreat of welfare state support and privatised public services. This already exacerbated the divide between the poles of British society; Covid-19 simply made matters worse. As we argue in the conclusion to this book, a progressive public policy is desperately needed to avert a humanitarian crisis unfolding in the UK.

To remind ourselves of the vicious impact of the trade-off between universal welfare and targeted financial market crisis support we sketch key stylised examples of where economic and social policy overlap and connect to everyday life. Namely, how living conditions of the poor in the UK have deteriorated over time, how Covid-19 found fertile ground in claiming the lives and livelihoods of those on low incomes and living in deprived areas. As we have argued throughout this book, policy decisions are not simply technocratic. Government responses to the pandemic demonstrated clearly how policy choices can be made *ideologically* rather than (primarily) *economically* driven. Yet, we must remain conscious of what is at stake: it is nothing less than 'the willingness of the UK government to feed its hungry children, to finance the NHS, and to invest in a just transition to a green economy' (Gabor 2020). Thus, the political economy of the pandemic response is about the social outcomes of decisions made by government policymakers.

5.2   No Homes—Insecure Housing for Non-Asset Holders

After decades of promoting asset-based welfare, residential housing has become a key financial asset for the middle and the top of the wealth distribution, while privatisation and austerity led to a large market-dominated and small public housing rental market in the UK. When the pandemic economic policy response deliberately targeted and insulated homeowners, it also made non-homeowners worse-off and more insecure. For the homeless, their experience was far more precarious.

5.2.1   *Renters in a Rentier Society*

A key pillar of the UK's Beveridge welfare state was ending squalor, which meant the government guaranteeing secure good-quality residential housing. However, the retreat of the welfare state brought the financialisation of housing and housing-based welfare. The key message for the poor was that, as non-asset owners, any support measures were meagre and temporary. This remained the policy stance in the pandemic economic response, from temporary eviction bans to emergency Universal Credit uplift.

Since the late 1990s the extent and role of the private rented sector in the UK has grown significantly, with 19% of all households in 2018/19 renting from a private landlord (compared to only 10% in 1997) (Joseph Roundtree Foundation 2021b: 10). At the same time the diversity of those renting has increased, with families with children the largest growing group (Cromarty 2020). Indeed, in late 2021 it was reported that Covid frontline workers—such as nurses, bus drivers, or senior care workers—were priced out of homeownership in 98% of UK cities (Duncan et al. 2021). This is a stark reality for hourly-paid waged workers, they are not paid enough to live where they work. This indicates a long-term need for rented accommodation among low-paid key workers. These low-paid workers are among a substantial proportion of private renters in general, those 'who have higher housing costs', and social renters, 'who tend to have lower incomes' (Joseph Roundtree Foundation 2021b: 3). Insecure employment coupled with insecure housing creates the very conditions of squalor and insecurity the welfare state once sought to eliminate but which are resurfacing acutely during a public health crisis.

Poor housing conditions are a long-standing public policy issue in the UK. 'The English Housing Survey Estimates that in 2018, 25% of homes in the Private Rented Sector in England were in a condition that would fail the Decent Homes Standard – around 1.2 million homes' (Cromarty 2020: 5). According to the charity Shelter (2021), 'Conditions in the sector are worse than in any other tenure, with 50% of homes not meeting basic government decency standards....' and here in particular the houses where the poorest live are most severely affected by bad housing conditions. With the shock of the pandemic and everyone ordered to stay at home, it was brought to the forefront how important safe accommodation in general is for health and well-being. 'Transmissible diseases thrive in poorly ventilated, poorly built, crowded dwellings. Physical and social structures intersect and co-produce vulnerability, mimicking the entanglements of and often resulting in syndemics. Poor housing compromises health; poor health impacts employment; loss of employment depletes income; low-income results in housing insecurity; and so on' (Team and Manderson 2020: 671).

So, the key message, in relation to our argument about asset-based welfare, is that poorer households, living in private rented accommodation, were particularly vulnerable in both health/social and economic terms. Data show strong correlations between death rates and areas with high prevalence of overcrowded housing, according to an Inside Housing study: having at least one bedroom less than required for the people living within the property promoted the spread of coronavirus (Inside Housing 2020). Meagre, temporary fiscal measures by the UK government did little to alleviate these vulnerabilities. Moreover, if the Bank of England messaging—of limitless funds and far-reaching efforts—served to reassure financial markets and asset owners, government messages on the other hand—of provisional, derisory measures merely amplified the anxieties of the poor.

Housing insecurity was dealt with directly by government with a temporary eviction ban and order to halt all court hearings on evictions until September 2020. A snapshot of housing insecurity at the outbreak of the pandemic in the UK indicates that 200,000 private renting households (5%) had fallen behind on their rent and 700,000 (15%) had fallen behind on bills such as council tax and utilities (Baxter et al. 2020); while 95,370 households were registered as homeless and living in temporary accommodation at the beginning of 2021. This marked a 7% increase from the 88,310 recorded at the end of 2019, meaning 7,060 more families lost their homes (The Metro 2021a). Early in May 2020, the government announced that renters would be further protected by a 'pre-action protocol', which encouraged landlords to work with their tenants to find a reasonable payment plan (Joseph Roundtree Foundation 2021a: 61). But the key point—for our purposes—is that these measures were temporary and were removed in May 2021.

More alarmingly, as fuel and energy costs rocketed in the second half of 2021 (see below), a crisis of rented accommodation loomed. By late 2021, the charity Step Change found that approximately 280,000 private renters were expecting to be forced out of their homes by the end of 2021, while 150,000 private renters were worried that they would be evicted due to rent arrears (incurred during Covid-19) in the next 12 months (StepChange 2021). The Trust for London reported that by late 2021, 6–7% of tenants were in arrears, nearly twice the normal rate. Meanwhile some 10% of private tenants were thought to be unemployed, about double the average rate (Trust for London 2021). Indeed, in the period from July to September 2021, the first full quarter since the ban on bailiff actions was lifted, there was a 207% increase in landlord repossessions (*The Guardian* 2021b). As the UK prepared to enter 2022, it seemed that the legacy of the pandemic for the poorest renters would involve mass evictions and increased homelessness, and a winter of uncertainty and fear.

5.2.2   *Homelessness*

This overview of the ways that asset-based welfare affected poorer renters' dovetails into a discussion of homelessness during the pandemic. One of the first governmental acts, as part of the stay-at-home order across all four nations of the UK, was to find self-contained accommodation for rough sleepers. It was reported that up to 15,000 people were housed during the pandemic. After a decade of austerity, homelessness and rough sleeping increased without any meaningful intervention from central government or local councils. Media reports represent the scale of the problem, between 2010 and 2016 the charity Crisis estimated that homelessness had increased by 132% (Homelessness Monitor 2017: viii) and figures from Shelter suggested that 23,000 people became homeless between 2016 and 2019, resulting in a homeless population of 280,000 people by the end of 2019 (Shelter 2019). Figures for London alone showed an increase of 35% of people sleeping rough between 2017 and 21 (*The Guardian* 2021c). As the pandemic hit, councils in England saw a 20% rise in people needing support for homelessness due to unemployment (The Big Issue 2021). As housing became an ever more lucrative financial asset for those at the top and the middle, those at the bottom struggle to secure any housing and many are not able to and end up sleeping on the street without adequate shelter.

Still much of the homeless population remains hidden, for example those reliant on insecure housing strategies, like couch-surfing and other forms of temporary accommodations—which are not counted in the official figures but represent a pent-up need for secure housing for those on low incomes. There are also important gender and racial dynamics to homelessness. It is often assumed that homeless populations are made up of white men; yet people from BAME backgrounds are overrepresented in the homeless population and female homelessness tends to be more widespread within the hidden groups of homelessness (hidden by access to temporary accommodation) and therefore underreported (The Big Issue 2021). Current estimates based on data by the Department for Communities and Local Government suggest that as a result of the temporary pandemic housing measures, the rough sleeping population across the UK had decreased from a high of 4751 in 2017 to 2688 in 2020 (Homeless Monitor 2021). While such housing initiatives are clearly more than welcome, against the backdrop of the lack of action to tackle homelessness meaningfully before the pandemic, it seems equally likely that efforts in 2020 were not altogether altruistic and were driven instead by concerns that those without shelter increased risks of spreading the virus. At the very least, temporary housing measures for the worst cases did not constitute a departure from the asset-based welfare paradigm that guided social welfare policy.

Indeed, when looking at welfare and housing policy between 2007 and 2020 one might conclude that consecutive governments knowingly allowed for a rise in homelessness, supported by ongoing discourses of individual responsibility for well-being. While the Homeless Reduction Act of 2017 added statutory duties to prevent and/or relieve homelessness, it did so against the background of ever shrinking council budgets since 2007. The lack of funding to uphold the duties of the Act became clear in the Government's own review of the Housing Act with findings published in 2020. Here, 'half of the 24 English councils surveyed raised the lack of affordable housing as a significant challenge they faced in responding to the Act. This was a concern for 68% of London boroughs and 40% of other local authorities'. Furthermore, while this legislation increased local authority spending on homelessness since 2010, 'overall council spending on housing… dropped by 46% in real terms, with an even larger cutback in their Supporting People programmes (67%)' (Shelter 2019). The big promises to tackle homelessness were clearly contradicted by the lack of effective financial support delivered to Councils to meet the respective targets. In short, the measures were simply inadequate.

The rollout of Universal Credit—especially the housing element—had a significant impact on homelessness. Previous research on the rollout of Universal Credit suggested that 'on average, it led to an increase of 1.74

landlord repossession claims, 1.42 landlord repossession orders and 0.70 landlord repossession warrants within local authorities (per 10,000 rented dwellings)' (Hardie 2021: 225) thereby risking people's, or claimant's access shelter, or basic human security. Identifiable groups were either 'entirely excluded from support with their housing costs (if 18–21 and not subject to an exemption), or subject to Shared Accommodation Rate limits on eligible rents in the social as well as private rented sector' (Homelessness Monitor 2017: ix).

It is those groups most likely to struggle when approaching local housing associations with requests of re-housing, such as large families with more than two children or young single people, who are more severely affected by the erosion of a social safety net.

This range of examples of homelessness, cramped living conditions, and ill-suited rented accommodation reinforces the point that squalor is rife in the asset economy, that is because owning assets is the one safe route to welfare and well-being. While the pandemic brought emergency temporary measures—like the eviction ban—which were much needed, they were meaningless when they were withdrawn only to revert to individual responsibility and the narrative of responsibility for misfortune. This meant that as the economy recovered in late 2021, an impending evictions and homelessness crisis was appearing on the horizon. If only the plight of those without any assets and without access to safe shelter was at the forefront of welfare reform following the pandemic, we could begin to see a substantial waning of inequality in the UK.

5.3   No Food Means no Security

Beyond housing, the preservation of the asset-based welfare template which informed the UK government's response to the pandemic allowed food insecurity to worsen. Despite all the fiscal stimulus, like the 'Eat Out to Help Out' scheme, a growing number of groups in society have struggled to eat properly during the pandemic. They struggled precisely because of the minimal government support for tackling food poverty, instead relying on community organisation to deliver charity-based food aid. 'The Trussell Trust reported a 122% rise in emergency food parcels given to children from food banks in their network during the second half of March 2020, compared to the same period in 2019' (Bibby et al. 2020: 7). Some commentators suggested that during the first lockdown the demand for emergency food support had quadrupled (Barker and Russell

2020). The Guardian reported in March 2021 that nine in ten councils had witnessed a significant rise in foodbank use during the pandemic with rises unequally distributed across the country. 'In Bradford three times as much food was distributed from 21 sites during the peak of the demand, compared to pre-Covid levels' (*The Guardian* 2021d). When Covid-19 struck, the outcome was—in many cases—the poorest in society experienced increased starvation.

Importantly, what became clear is the degree to which postal code inequalities within the UK, at the regional and local levels, perpetuate food insecurity. The increased demand for emergency food support during Covid also occurred against the background of already heightened vulnerabilities in accessing food caused by ongoing austerity politics since 2010 (Lamie-Mumford and Green 2017). Existing inequalities in access to food, and in particular access to 'good' food, depended on where one lives. Here, the geography of deprivation is stark: 26% of the children in North-East England qualify for free school meals, compared to 15% in the South-East (The Big Issue 2021). Reported evidence suggests the main drivers of food insecurity are the 'lack of financial security, including unemployment, household debt, and weaknesses in the state benefits system' (Barker and Russell 2020: 865). A report by Human Rights Watch in 2019, documented the detrimental impact on food security of poor families of fiscal austerity policies since 2010; the financial benefits cap, the freeze on most working age benefits, the two-child limit on child benefit, the rollout of the Universal Credit (UC) system, as responsible for this effect. There is little doubt that central government cuts, or policy choices, were the ultimate source of these changes. One report detailed the 'clear link between the restructuring of the welfare system and a marked increase in food poverty among low-income families who receive such support' (HRW 2019). In 2018, it was estimated that the UK had the highest level of food insecurity in Europe (FAO 2018), which was later confirmed by findings of a British Medical Journal report again in 2019 (BMJ 2019). Therefore, it must be acknowledged that food insecurity is a persistent problem in the UK, exacerbated by the pandemic despite the scale of both fiscal and monetary measures.

Arguably the best indicator of the rate of emergency food support distributed throughout the UK came from the Trussell Trust (2021) a charity that runs the largest network of UK food banks: they highlighted a 5146% increase in emergency food parcels handed out between 2008 and 2018, from 26,000 to more than 1.33 million, there was an 11% increase in food bank usage between April and September 2021, compared to the same period in 2019 (Trussell Trust 2021). Yet, it is not only the access to food per se that was severely limited for poor people, access to 'good' food was even more compromised for people on low incomes. NHS figures published in November 2021 revealed—for example—those cases of malnutrition had almost doubled in the decade since the Conservatives came to power (The Metro 2021b). In 2010 there were 4,657 cases of people being treated in hospital for the condition; by 2020 it had risen to 10,109.

Furthermore, research from the University of Sheffield suggested that 10.2 million people in the UK live in areas where access to fresh fruit and vegetables is too expensive given limited budgets and respective transport costs (UoS 2018). Such so-called food deserts extend into nearly one in 10 of the country's most economically deprived areas, where supermarkets and reasonably priced shops are absent, and communities are only served by corner shops where fruit and vegetables are expensive or not sold at all. This puts the poor, elderly, and disabled people as disproportionately affected by lack of access to affordable transport and, thus, food security.

What is particularly startling however, is that the economy re-opened and people returned to work in late 2021, food insecurity for the poorest continued to increase. Thus, we concur with Lombardozzi et al. who show that 'food insecurity…. should not be analysed as an ad-hoc, unpredictable and contingent phenomena, but rather linked to structural determinants such as deflationary policy on wages (which define household and individual purchasing power), restrictive regulatory system on physical spaces, and lack of fair access to resources and institutional knowledge on how to navigate the "system" to enable food provision for all' (2021: 4–5). It was reported by Alison Garnham, chief executive of Child Poverty action group, that approximately 5100 food packages were handed out daily in October–November 2021, to which she emphasised, 'No parent wants to have to rely on charity to feed their kids but the value of social security has fallen so low that the choice for many – including low-income earners – is eat food parcels or don't eat all… unless we restore our social security system, more children will be pushed into poverty and more families will be deprived of dignity' (as reported in The Mirror 2021).

Put simply, those without assets found themselves homeless (or close to) and malnourished (or starving), as asset-based welfare had meant the removal of the public safety net intended to provide government support to those most vulnerable members of society.

5.4   Poor Children and the Moral Economy of Deprivation

The protection of children from deprivation was a key injustice addressed by the formation of the welfare state. When the Covid-19 pandemic struck, the lack of medical danger for children from the virus obscured the profoundly negative impact the virus and the political response had on young people. Among the most vulnerable social groups, children deserve a special mention because of the acute and devastating impact of the pandemic on them.

Child poverty is defined in the UK as children growing up in households that have less than 60% of the median wage available to live on. Between 2014 and 19 the level of children growing up in poverty increased by 12.5 percentage points, marking the biggest increase in child poverty ever; the cumulative outcomes are a staggering 30% of UK children growing up in poverty. Child poverty levels differ regionally, with Tower Hamlets leading the way with 55.4% of children growing up poor (Valadez and Hirsch 2018), and with Birmingham having the highest level of child poverty outside London with 41.6%. Just to allow the full weight of those figures to sink in: 30% of UK children equates to approximately 4.3 million children and young people that experience the devastating reality of living in poverty. Also, 'child poverty is on the rise. A recent National Education Union (NEU) member survey found that over half of respondents have seen an increase in child poverty at their school or college since March 2020, the start of the first national lockdown. The latest research from the Resolution Foundation predicts that by the next General Election, 730,000 more children and young people will be caught in poverty's grip' (NEU 2021).

The intersectionalities of inequalities around childhood poverty are also painfully obvious. 49% of single parent families are poor, children from black and ethnic minority backgrounds are disproportionately affected by poverty, and the poverty rate for families with disabled family members has been on the rise since 2011/12 (NEU 2021). With child poverty already increasing before the pandemic, during the pandemic access to money and other resources became ever more scarce for struggling families. According to a report by the Child Poverty Action Group and the

Church of England from December 2020 'eight in 10 low-income families with children had experienced a significant deterioration in their living standards as a result of coronavirus, caused by a combination of a drop in income and rising costs' (p. 3).

Class differences have a damaging impact on families already struggling to get by. Without a strong safety net an unexpected job loss or losses of earnings due to hours being cut is just the start of a downward spiral. With Covid-19 lockdowns came homeschooling and its associated costs to those who cared for those children, whether lost earnings or social isolation. Closures of child and other care support structures hit those already in poverty the hardest, which had a devastating impact on children.

Beyond the *financial* effects of the pandemic, children in poor families were disproportionately affected by non-financial effects. While all children were affected by the disruption to their schooling, those from poorer families were hit hardest with 'long term effects on their educational progression and labour market performance. Younger generations have experienced disrupted education and they face a tougher labour market than that seen prior to the pandemic' (Blundell et al. 2020: 3). But child poverty also has outcomes beyond the childhood years. Indeed, according to the NHS Scotland (2018) report on the health impact and health inequalities of child poverty, 'the negative impacts of poverty on children start before birth and accumulate across the life course' (p. 1). While poverty is connected to a range of factors negatively impacting the affected child's life outcomes, including lack of social security, lack of flexible work, availability of childcare, the very 'lack of money' available to families 'has shown to have the strongest impact on children's cognitive, social-behavioural, educational attainment and health outcomes, independent of other factors such as parents' education' (NHS Scotland 2018: 1). What matters most is the overlap between the social, cognitive, emotional, health, developmental, behavioural, and educational outcomes which all coalesce within the purview of the welfare state.

Having already dealt with food insecurity in general, we return to hunger as one of the most devastating consequences of child poverty. Poor children in the UK have limited access to food, outside of state-funded school meals, but the quality is bad which means there is limited access to good-quality food, which is extremely concerning. From a public health perspective, it is well established that '(p)overty and poor diets are inextricably linked and lead to poor health outcomes such as obesity and nutrition-related chronic diseases. The prevalence of malnutrition, which includes overweight and obesity as well as underweight and stunting in children, and poor dental health are worse in children living in poorer households. Rates of obesity amongst 4–5-year olds in the most deprived areas are double those in the least deprived areas. Poor diets low in food variety are more likely to be low in essential micronutrients necessary for growth and development, and are associated with children missing meals' (Moore and Evans 2020: 2). As mentioned above the child food poverty crisis only worsened during the pandemic as families were forced to provide meals at home that were previously provided by schools and after-school care.

The initiative championed by the Manchester United footballer Marcus Rashford and the government U-Turn it forced—to extend free school meals during school holidays—very publicly highlighted the plight of families on the breadline (The Metro 2021c). The U-Turn provided temporary reprieve for those families reliant on—for example—holiday club programmes, which were closed during lockdowns. But the underlying causes of child food poverty remained unaddressed. As O'Connell et al. (2018: 1) highlighted, food aid was an inadequate response that is 'susceptible to four particular challenges: it can be inaccessible, unreliable, unaccountable, and socially unacceptable'. Indeed, as late as September 2021 the (cross-party) House of Commons Work and Pensions Select Committee noted that, 'at the moment, the government has no strategy and no measurable objectives against which it can be held to account. How [then] can it hope to reduce child poverty when it doesn't have a plan?' (cited in *The Guardian* 2021c). If the template for governmental policies during the pandemic essentially emphasised protecting asset owners and providing temporary relief (before a return to individualised responsibility) for the most vulnerable, then this blueprint is perhaps most apparent of all in the devastating affects felt by poor and underprivileged children.

5.5 No Money and the Compounding Problem of Precarity

In Chapter 4 we mapped out the difference between the balance sheet and the budget sheet in the asset economy. Asset owners, middle-income homeowners for example, might be asset rich; and therefore, on paper, their balance sheets look healthy due to housing equity. On the other hand, even middle-income homeowners have squeezed budget sheets, referring to their challenges in managing monthly incomings and outgoings. For the poorest non-asset owners, their 'financial resilience – the ability of families to cope with a fall in income – was [already] poor' prior to Covid (Resolution Foundation 2021b: 10); as the IFS (2021: 7) noted, 'the years leading up to the COVID19 crisis…had left many households in a precarious position'; and the budget sheet crisis of the poorest households only escalated during the pandemic. There were at least three important drivers of this crisis in household finances for the poor: the impact of Covid-19 on their working conditions; the temporary nature of the governmental financial support; and the cost-of-living crisis.

Firstly, Covid-19 disproportionately impacted working conditions for the poor. As furlough packages were launched early in the pandemic, and the government encouraged individuals to work from home, middle-income homeowners saw—on average—savings increase, house prices rise, and working conditions improve (Resolution Foundation 2021b: 21). In stark contrast those working in non-food retail, hospitality, and leisure were heavily affected. According to a Social Metrics Commission report (2020), 81% of those working in hospitality and leisure were negatively financially impacted. In fact, 98% of elementary workers (cleaners, retail sales assistants, bus drivers, carers, delivery drivers, and so forth) were unable to work from home. And those workers tend to come from the lowest income social groups. The result was that 'workers in the lowest income quintile had the largest drop-in mean hours worked' (Joseph Roundtree Foundation 2021a: 32).

Secondly, the government financial support for the poor was limited and temporary, just as it had been with the evictions ban. Between March and December 2020 there was a 90% increase in claimants of universal credit (Joseph Roundtree Foundation 2020). Partially in response, the government introduced a £20 a week increase in universal credit and working tax credit for families in April 2020. Analysis by the Joseph Roundtree Foundation late in 2020, showed that 6.2 million families were critically dependent on the £20 uplift, with 500,000 people at risk of being swept into poverty were it to be removed (ibid.). Already the £20 uplift had been shrouded in controversy though, with disabled people being denied the additional funds because the government contended that 'it would be too complicated for its computer system to process' their claims (The Independent 2020). Nonetheless, surveys showed that a majority (59%) of the public supported making the universal credit increase permanent (Ipsos MORI 2020). By late 2020 however, the Conservative government was reiterating the message that the financial support package for the poorest in society would be removed at some point in 2021.

What made matters worse was that as the pandemic unfolded, the impact on household finances for the lowest income groups became increasingly apparent. This makes the government's refusal to maintain the £20 uplift even more unacceptable. Headline figures show that—in the aggregate—households increased savings by around £125bn (Resolution Foundation 2021a: 5). But—digging below the surface—it became clear that 'changes in debt were [heavily] skewed' (ibid.). Citizen's Advice (2021) estimated for example, that 6 million adults had fallen behind on at least one household bill over the course of the pandemic. The Office for National Statistics highlighted that by December 2020 nearly 9 million people had to borrow more money than usual, 'with lower income groups, self-employed and people who rent accommodation most affected' (ONS 2021). Indeed, even a UK Parliament report was forced to concede that 'there is evidence to suggest that some households, particularly those with low incomes, have run down savings and increased debt since the start of the pandemic' (Houses of Parliament 2021). This led the Resolution Foundation to contend that 'the distribution of debt and savings changes provides extra justification for keeping the pandemic support of an additional £20 per week to Universal Credit (UC); those in receipt of UC are low income and are less likely to have increased savings and more likely to have increased debt' (Resolution Foundation 2021b: 9).

Despite strong public support to keep UC uplift permanently though, the October 2021 Budget cut the £20 supplement. The *quid pro quo*, at least as far as the government explained it, was that there would be an increase in the living wage from £8.91 to £9.50 per hour. The idea behind increasing the living wage harkens back to our discussion of the dependence on waged income from the labour market coupled with individualised responsibility for social security. The Chancellor, Rishi Sunak MP, described his budget as the one for the 'age of optimism', forecasting increased productivity, economic recovery, and new and better paid jobs (CityAm 2021). In line with this blue sky, utopian thinking, the government felt no need to increase the welfare safety net for those least able to cope with the economic shock. Rather, the poorest were told that more jobs and higher wages would at some point be available to meet those needs. But this view was highly contested. Critics argued that the 'coronavirus pandemic has exacerbated the pre-existing barriers to work as a route out of poverty' (Joseph Roundtree Foundation 2021b: 37). The deputy director of the Joseph Roundtree Foundation for example, argued that 'It is completely wrong to suggest there is a trade-off between good jobs and adequate social security when they are both essential to improving people's living standards' (The Big Issue 2021).

Thirdly however, against the backdrop of the rising cost-of-living crisis analysts predicted that the gap between anticipated wages and the cuts to universal credit would plunge many households even further into poverty. Already analysis by the Institute for Fiscal Studies showed that 'the cocktail of high inflation, tepid pay growth and sharp tax rises' meant that despite the headline boosts to public spending emphasised by the government, UK households are set to face 'years of stagnating living standards' (*FT* 2021). But it is also widely recognised that poorer households pay higher living costs (as a proportion of their income) and, on average, have higher energy costs (in real terms) as well (The Independent 2021). Figures showed for example, that Britain's poorest 10% of households pay on average £756 a year per person for electricity, gas, and other fuels, compared with an average of £504 per person in the richest households. Rising inflation and the energy crisis of late 2021 therefore had a disproportionate impact on the household finances of the poor.

As Marion Fellows MP put it: 'underprivileged families have been an afterthought in this budget. It looks like a long, hard winter for so many people, who must now choose between the heating and eating' (cited in UK Parliament 2021). Indeed, research conducted by the University of York showed that 3.4 million households, or 6.3 million adults and children, would not be able to pay rising gas and electricity bills in the winter of 2021 without cutting their food spending (Sky 2021). In short, the temporary assistance offered to poorer households, followed by the return to promises of jobs and wages in place of government welfare support, simply returned the poorest households to living conditions devastated first by austerity and then by the pandemic.

5.6   Closing Thoughts

This is a book about the new fault lines of inequality in the UK. According to the Institute for Fiscal Studies, 'it is clear…that the COVID19 pandemic has enhanced existing inequalities and brought to the fore other inequalities that were perhaps less of a concern prior to the pandemic' (IFS 2021: 24). Therefore, we recognise these fault lines, or ruptures in the social and economic fabric of society, are caused in large part by the policies of the asset economy pursued by successive UK governments. The poorest—the non-asset owners—the social groups highlighted in this chapter have benefited neither from the increase in asset prices during the pandemic, nor from significant and permanent welfare support from the state. Arguments about limits of state spending as a justification for the temporary measures offered to the poor are hard to reconcile with the evidence of almost unlimited state spending and central-bank asset-purchase programmes invoked to stabilise and reinvigorate financial markets.

Instead, what is much more plausible is that the government rhetoric of limits on state spending used to justify the ending the UC £20 uplift and initially denying free school meals, provide further evidence of the privatised Keynesian policy paradigm. In the absence of access to welfare via assets, all that is left for the poor is individualised responsibility for deprivation and misfortune. But, as we know, work—even full-time well-paid work—provides no guarantees of a way out of poverty. Even prior to the pandemic, 43% of children of one-earner couples lived in relative poverty, and more than 30% of couple households with one full-time earner lived in poverty (IFS 2017: 7). Yet, high paid jobs will be available, at least if Rishi Sunak is to be believed, leaving the only option to work your way out of poverty in an asset economy.

Inequality can be improved or worsened by political decisions. In an asset economy, a privatised Keynesian policy regime is where state managers focus on the expansion of central-bank balance sheets on asset purchases rather than on fiscal transfers and services to households. Immediately, some readers will balk at the idea of depositing cash directly into the bank accounts of households. It should be noted here however, that the Bank of England's own research found that money finance transfers could stimulate spending and economic recovery in much the same way as bond financing could. It doesn't stop there: what research has shown over and over, is that the one thing that can improve the health, well-being, and life chances of the poor is money. Studies of programmes of universal payments to households in Finland found improved levels of mental, physical, and financial well-being for recipients (Finland Ministry of Social Affairs and Health 2019); while researchers in Canada also proposed a basic income pilot on the basis that it could reduce domestic violence (Mulvale and Delaney 2006). Therefore, we must think anew about how to better deliver universal welfare to citizens in ways that will bring the conditions of those at 'the bottom' upwards, ending deprivation as housing or food insecurity is a good place to start.

References

Barker, M., and J. Russell. 2020. Feeding the food insecure in Britain: Learning from the 2020 COVID-19 crisis. *Food Security* 12: 865–870.

Baxter, D., R. Earwaker, and R. Casey. 2020. *Struggling renters need a lifeline.* York: Joseph Roundtree Foundation.

Bibby, J., G. Everest, and I. Abbs. 2020. Will Covid-19 be a watershed moment for health inequalities. *The Health Foundation.* https://www.health.org.uk/sites/default/files/2020-05/Will%20COVID-19%20be%20a%20watershed%20moment%20for%20health%20inequalities.pdf.

Blundell, R., R. Joyce, M.C. Dias, and X. Xu. 2020. *Covid-19: The impacts of the pandemic on inequality* [Briefing note]. Institute for Fiscal Studies (IFS).

BMJ. 2019. Food insecurity in UK is among worst in Europe, especially for children, says committee. *British Medical Journal* 364: 126–127.

Boris Johnson on Facebook 17 May 2020.

Boris Johnson, House of Commons Statement, 22 September 2020.

CityAM. 2021. Budget: Rishi Sunak's 'age of optimism' boosted by higher growth forecast post-Covid, 27 October.

Cromarty, H. 2020. *Housing conditions in the private rented sector (England).* House of Commons Briefing Paper No. 7328, 4 February.

Duncan, et al. 2021. https://www.theguardian.com/uk-news/2021/mar/30/covid-frontline-workers-priced-out-of-homeowning-in-98-of-great-britain.

Finland Ministry of Social Affairs. 2019. Preliminary Results of the Basic Income Experiment: Self-perceived wellbeing improved, during the first year no effects on employment. https://stm.fi/en/-/perustulokokeilun-alustavat-tulokset-hyvinvointi-koettiin-paremmaksi-ensimmaisena-vuonna-ei-tyollisyysvaikutuksia.

Financial Times. 2021. COVID19: Widening the gap between rich and poor, 16 February.

Food and Agricultural Organisation (FAO). 2018. *The state of food security and nutrition in the world: Building climate resilience for food security and nutrition.* FAO: Rome.

Gabor, D. 2020. Why you shouldn't fall for the panic about Britain's public debt. *The Guardian.* https://www.theguardian.com/commentisfree/2020/oct/29/panic-britain-public-debt-government-borrowing-pandemic.

Hancock, Matt. 2021. BBC Breakfast, 13 January.

Hancock, Matt. 2020. BBC daily coronavirus address, 19 April.

Hardie, I. 2021. The impact of universal credit rollout on housing security: An analysis of landlord repossession rates in English local authorities. *Journal of Social Policy* 50 (2): 225–246. https://doi.org/10.1017/S00472794200 00021.

Homeless Monitor. 2021. Crisis. https://www.crisis.org.uk/ending-homelessn ess/homelessness-knowledge-hub/homelessness-monitor/england/the-hom elessness-monitor-england-2021/.

Homelessness Monitor. 2017. Crisis. https://www.crisis.org.uk/ending-hom elessness/homelessness-knowledge-hub/homelessness-monitor/england/the- homelessness-monitor-england-2017/.

Houses of Parliament. 2021. https://commonslibrary.parliament.uk/research-bri efings/cbp-9060/.

Human Rights Watch (HRW). 2019. https://www.hrw.org/report/2019/05/ 20/nothing-left-cupboards/austerity-welfare-cuts-and-right-food-uk.

IFS. 2017. In work poverty among families with children. Available at: https://ifs.org.uk/uploads/publications/comms/r129_ch5.pdf. Accessed 14 December 2021.

IFS. 2021. Inequalities in education, skills and incomes in the UK: The implications of the COVID19 pandemic, March.

Inside Housing. 2020. The housing pandemic: Four graphs showing the link between COVID-19 deaths and the housing crisis. https://www.insidehou sing.co.uk/insight/insight/the-housing-pandemic-four-graphs-showing-the- link-between-covid-19-deaths-and-the-housing-crisis-66562.

Ipsos MORI. 2020. Majority of public support making £20 per week Universal Credit uplift permanent, 18 December.

Joseph Roundtree Foundation. 2020. Coalition warns it would be a terrible mistake to cut the £20 uplift to Universal Credit, 29 November.

Joseph Roundtree Foundation. 2021a. The Living Standards Outlook 2021, January.

Joseph Roundtree Foundation. 2021b. *UK Poverty 2020–21, the leading independent report*. London: Joseph Roundtree Foundation.

Lamie, H., and A. Green. 2017. Austerity, welfare reform and the rising use of food banks by children in England and Wales. *Area* 49 (3): 273–279.

Moore, B., and C. Evans. 2020. Tackling Childhood Food Poverty in the UK. Leed Policy Briefs. https://eprints.whiterose.ac.uk/168869/1/PolicyLeeds- Brief4_Childhood-Food-Poverty.pdf.

Mulvale, J., and D. Delaney. 2006. *Advancing economic security for women through basic income: Soundings in Saskatchewan*. Regina: Provincial Association of Transition Houses and Services of Saskatchewan.

National Education Union (NEU). 2021. Child Poverty. https://neu.org.uk/ press-releases/child-poverty.

NHS Scotland. 2018. 4. Child Poverty in Scotland: Health impact and health inequalities. NHS. http://www.healthscotland.scot/media/2186/child-poverty-impact-inequalities-2018.pdf.

O'Connell, R., J. Brannen, and A. Knight. 2018. https://blogs.bmj.com/bmj/2018/08/15/holiday-hunger-requires-radical-long-term-solutions/.

ONS. 2021. Personal and economic well-being in Great Britain: January 2021. Available at: https://www.ons.gov.uk/peoplepopulationandcommunity/wellbeing/bulletins/personalandeconomicwellbeingintheuk/january2021#savings-borrowing-and-affordability. Accessed 14 December 2021.

Resolution Foundation. 2021a. (Wealth) Gap Year: The impact of the coronavirus crisis on UK household wealth, July.

Resolution Foundation. 2021b. After Shocks: Financial resilience before and during the COVID19 crisis, April.

Shelter. 2019. This is England: A picture of Homelessness in 2019. https://england.shelter.org.uk/professional_resources/policy_and_research/policy_library/this_is_england_a_picture_of_homelessness_in_2019.

Shelter. 2021. Denied the right to a safe home: Factsheet. https://england.shelter.org.uk/professional_resources/policy_and_research/policy_library/denied_the_right_to_a_safe_home_factsheet.

Sky. 2021. Cut to universal credit uplift 'not the right way to save government money' says Gordon Brown, 4 October.

Social Metrics Commission. 2020. Measuring Poverty 2020. https://socialmetricscommission.org.uk/measuring-poverty-2020/.

StepChange. 2021. Preventing a COVID arrears crisis: Financial support package for renters, 27 May.

Team, V., and L. Manderson. 2020. How COVID-19 Reveals Structures of Vulnerability. *Medical Anthropology* 39 (8): 671–674. https://doi.org/10.1080/01459740.2020.1830281

The Big Issue. 2021. Thousands became homeless during pandemic with more feared in Autumn, 9 September.

The Guardian. 2021a. Renter activists block London eviction as end of COVID protections takes toll, 24 November.

The Guardian. 2021b. Rise in women sleeping rough is hidden in England, charities warn, 30 June.

The Guardian. 2021c. Ministers have no clear plan to tackle child poverty, say cross-party MPs, 22 September.

The Guardian. 2021d. More than 1m children from key worker families living in poverty, says TUC, 14 July.

The Independent. 2020. Disabled people denied benefit uplift during pandemic because it would be "too complicated" for DWP IT system, 18 November.

The Independent. 2021. People living in poverty 'hit harder by gas and electricity bills', new data shows, 24 October.

The Metro. 2021a. Almost 100,000 families were homeless at the beginning of 2021, 22 April.

The Metro. 2021b. Malnutrition doubles to over 10,000 cases under Tory rule, 8 November.

The Metro. 2021c. Marcus Rashford forces another government U-Turn on free school meals, 8 November.

The Mirror. 2021. Foodbanks hand out 32 meals every minute—And it's about to get worse, 24 November.

Trussell Trust. 2021. More than 5,100 food parcels given to people facing crisis across the UK every day in past six months, says the Trussell Trust, 24 November.

UK Parliament. 2021. Income Tax (charge): Volume 702, debated on Thursday 28 October 2021. Daily Hansard.

University of Sheffield. 2018. https://www.sheffield.ac.uk/social-sciences/news/12-million-living-uk-food-deserts-studys-shows

Valadez, L., and D. Hirsch. 2018. *Child Poverty map of the UK January 2018*. London: End Child Poverty Coalition.

CHAPTER 6

Conclusion

Abstract The conclusion summarises the implications of the Covid-19 pandemic on inequality in the UK. The book argued that support for the asset economy and the policy blueprint of privatised Keynesianism have worsened inequality. Indeed, the UK economic policy response to the pandemic has, despite unprecedented amounts of funding, driven the fault lines of society further apart. Building on this critique of the policy response, we argue for a new thinking around inequality and propose a direction of travel for economic and social policy. A care-led and green economy policy paradigm informed by Keynesian spending incentives can in the short run address some of the worst consequences of inequality. Redistributive taxation and spending decisions are easily implemented and can build on a blueprint of post-war universal welfare ideals to help reverse some of the worst suffering and hardship. Yet, in the medium term we believe more transformative politics are needed that truly take account of the multifaceted nature of inequality and go beyond technocratic fixes in order to develop a more human and equal society in the long run.

Keywords Inequality · Progressive · Distribution · Levelling up · Renewed Keynesianism

© The Author(s), under exclusive license to Springer Nature Switzerland AG 2022
H. Macartney et al., *The Fault Lines of Inequality*,
https://doi.org/10.1007/978-3-030-96914-1_6

This book has explored the impact the economic response to the Covid-19 pandemic had on inequality in the UK. We argued that the defining feature of the UK economy is the asset economy, and this is consistently supported by a policy blueprint of 'privatised' Keynesianism. Indeed, it is this combination, we argue, that caused worsening inequality as a result of the Covid-19 pandemic. State policymakers' consistent (and almost unlimited) protection of asset markets, which benefit only the wealthiest in society, compared to means-tested and temporary emergency measures for everyone else are the forces driving the poles in society further apart. We set about showing how policy decisions to prioritise the asset economy increased the wealth at the top, provided a temporary stopgap for the 'squeezed' middle, and continued emergency welfare provision for the bottom strata of society. Here, trends were not simply kept the same, policy decisions worsened the chasm between social groups. Yet, all of this is not new. The UK's economic response to the pandemic mirrors in substantial parts economic policy decisions in the wake of the financial crisis of 2008—these continuous policies are exacerbating inequality further. The status of the UK as one of the most unequal societies in the industrialised world is hereby further cemented.

6.1   THE PROBLEM WITH THE RETURN TO NORMAL

So far, we have covered the headline economic response policies implemented as part of the UK government's Covid-19 pandemic response. These were always framed as only temporary measures but have now given way to a clear impetus of a return to normal. As we have shown, 'normal' means returning to the same inequality creating asset economy—just without emergency measures—which is a defining feature of UK society that will only worsen. Normal means the fault lines of society thus are permitted to stay unchallenged.

The UK Parliamentary Committee (2021) report, 'COVID: Lessons learned to date' stated that politicians and civil servants abandoned the precautionary principle designed to protect people, instead choosing to respond to the virus through a 'veil of ignorance' about its potential negative effects. The UK government drew direct equivalences between the business losses incurred with the losses to human life, without any meaningful opposition; routinely using the 'economic costs of the health care system' as needing to be minimised, despite the continued loss of human life. In July 2021, the UK government abandoned all temporary public health measures and dubbed it 'Freedom Day' in the name of 'returning to normality' for the economy, rather than for the health of the nation. And never has this message been clearer than in discussions around new public health measures or lockdown in Christmas/New Year 2021/22 due to the Omicron variant. While most of the western world has decided to implement clear and strict measures against the spread of Omicron, the UK's Conservative government is resolute in reducing public health measures because they infringe on people's 'rights', especially the right to party and mingle (which seems to have never been restricted within No.10's inner circle!). Here, the belief that 'normal' means no government involvement in supporting the wider health of the public is resurfacing. Much like the Conservatives' austerity agenda, there is a clear retreat of the state from supporting the well-being of a large part of its population. Insisting on normal being restored is the latest articulation of the subordinate role of public health and well-being in the UK social settlement.

Let us be clear, any measures can be seen as a threat to economic prosperity (if that is how you view systemic stability) and thus must be rolled back, even if it means higher infections and deaths. Reaching 150,000 deaths in January 2022—the worst human life loss in Europe due to Covid—has barely raised an eyebrow in government.

What has become clear is the degree to which the Conservative party, and other elected officials, as well as the civil service, have abandoned the precautionary principle of protecting civilian populations from illness and potential death when faced with potential economic losses to the domestic economy. We hasten to add these same concerns do not guide Brexit policy occurring at the same time, in which years of economic losses are dismissed as worth the gains to political sovereignty. While we are not offering an analysis of Brexit, we nevertheless have to recognise they are happening at the same time; UK government policymaking does not need to be coherent or complimentary to have an overlapping impact on its citizens. The similarity we do recognise though is a callous disregard for the well-being of citizens and a quiet acceptance of widening inequality.

6.2   Redressing Inequality in Policy and Politics

What is underlying all this talk of normality is a mindset where flawed economic ideas remain unchallenged within government policymaking, further perpetuating social ills. Dominant economic ideas about the domestic or macro-economy are built on the flawed notion that inequality will reduce over time due to gains in technology and market efficiency. This is significant to our analysis because of the influence and dominance of economic ideas within the policymaking domain. We follow Earle et al.'s (2016) post-2008 crisis reflection on the power of Economics in UK policymaking in their book, *The Econocracy*, which outlines how economic expertise in public policy is shaped by authority, rather than legitimacy: 'Economic knowledge gives the experts who hold it claims to know how the economy works and therefore to shape our collective views about its health, design policies to improve it and pass judgement on the economic competence of businesses, political parties and whole nations' (p. 9). Applying this insight to the pandemic economic response, demonstrates why a return to normal is a particularly dangerous path to take. To put it rather bluntly: a misleading view of inequality brings inappropriate policies which, as the pandemic confirms, lead to further suffering and deprivation in society.

We concur with Ian Goldin (2021) when he argues 'what is required now is *not* (highlighted by authors) a bouncing back from the pandemic to what we had before, or a reset to the pre-Covid operating system. Unless we reduce the growing inequalities within our countries and between them, we are heading towards a bleak future'. Technocratic perceptions of neutrality only aggravate, rather than resolve, the underlying challenges facing humanity. A bleak future awaits if inequality is allowed to break down the fabric of society itself beyond repair - as the poles are driven further apart, social cohesion becomes impossible. As such, failure to address inequality exacerbates the misfortune caused by the Covid-19 pandemic, leading towards a bleak future.

In different words, we need a *new normal*. We are encouraged in this endeavour by economists and policymakers who challenge existing thinking on inequality (Mian et al. 2021). Indeed, to avoid pessimism and fatalism in this conclusion we want to push beyond simply summarising potential outcomes. We have shown what has happened to those at the top, middle and bottom; now we want to propose a direction of travel.

6.3 Advancing a New Normal—Solutions for the Twenty-First Century

What is most surprising about the UK's economic policy response to the pandemic is that it made inequality worsen, as one would expect fiscal and monetary measures would have at least provided some generalised welfare. However, the scale of intervention only put a floor under the collapse of markets, which drove the existing poles in society further apart. The reality is simple, there are ample policy measures that can be adopted to reduce income and wealth inequality in the UK: from taxation, government investment, to a wide array of public services. Looking around the world or to history gives plenty of proven methods for reducing income and wealth inequality, the problem is the UK government does not want to follow these examples. Just like it was a choice during post-crisis austerity to reduce public services, so too is it a choice not to reverse inequality.

The good news is—economic inequality _can_ be addressed through a twenty-first-century Keynesian policy paradigm, such as that articulated in the green and care-led pandemic recovery paradigm (New Economy Brief 2021). However, this is in stark contrast to the current Conservative government's 'levelling up' agenda to tackle inequality. What is most striking about the levelling up agenda is the ease with which policy-makers can identify—as in locate geographically—deprived communities and regions without any meaningful ability or attempt to change them, because the structural conditions underlying poverty and inequality are ignored in favour of highly calibrated targeted responses.

Undoubtedly there is a compelling case to reverse the conditions that create inequality through policy choices. For example, the 'Green Care-led' Keynesian paradigm that would redress inequality; taxation and state investment should feature prominently in such an endeavour. Taking Piketty and others' framing of wealth inequality as basic 'rentierism', which means the form that income flows take—as returns from assets or employment—as central to configuring inequality. Following Keynes' conclusions from the General Theory, to 'euthanize the rentier' through low-interest rates, this principle is adapted for the current already low-interest environment to focus on wealth taxation, both globally and nationally. This adaptation addresses the unique features of the asset economy and the existing 'privatised' Keynesian paradigm that connects credit creation to asset-price inflation.

A wealth tax on 'unearned' income from economic rents is both a revenue source for the Treasury as well as a deterrent against profiteering from corporations operating the global financial architecture, and not even that contested among the global elite. Thus, a key element of addressing economic inequality is comprehensive tax reform: taxing wealth, including property wealth, in the same way as employment income. As one commentator noted, 'our extraordinary battle against the pandemic should draw on the immense reserves that the most privileged among us have accumulated over decades of abundance' (*NY Times* 2020). Moreover, as it became apparent that the wealth of the ultra-rich had multiplied so dramatically during the pandemic, calls for a COVID windfall tax increased. A YouGov UK survey of 1,682 people in May 2020 revealed that 61% would approve of a wealth tax for those with assets over £750,000 (*FT* 2020). Public opinion might be shifting, but the material realities of the concentration of wealth compared to the proliferation of deprivation are stark. Analysis funded by the *Guardian* (2021) reveals that low capital gains tax since 1990 has meant that those at the very top have been able to convert their income disproportionately from salaries to income from shares and properties, thus reducing their overall tax burden. Taxation is a key fault line of inequality and under the direct control of state managers.

When we focus in on policymakers in the Treasury, and their tax and spend decisions, we put state resource allocation at the centre of understanding inequality. A highly unequal tax burden for salaries (45% top income tax) and only 20% from shares and 28% from property income has protected the assets of the richest in society. Furthermore, the 'highly regressive' (Institute for Fiscal Studies 2020) taxation of properties in the UK in the form of council tax which has remained unchanged for the last 30 years are contributing to levels of regional inequality in the UK now outstripping that of East and West Germany at the time of unification, according to Philip McCann and Ortega-Argiles (2021). To put this into perspective, West Germans pay a solidarity contribution tax (*Solidaritätszuschlag*) of around 5.5% since 1991 (although this has been reformed since 2021 with only 6% of income earners still paying) that has been used to finance regional investments in the East of Germany that outstrip regional investment in the UK's poorer regions significantly.

These are measures that should be easy to enforce as policy guidelines as well as historical precedents exist. Agreeing to twenty-first-century principles for universal welfare provision is urgently needed. Narratives of individual responsibility for poverty must be replaced with a recognition of the structural determinants of inequality and an ethical commitment to end suffering.

Since the 2008 global financial crisis, there has been a revival of Keynesian economic ideas to inform alternatives to fiscal austerity and unconventional monetary policy which puts equity, well-being, and ecological sustainability at its core. We have seen a cornucopia of policy proposals to reform taxation, invest in green transformation, invest in social infrastructure, and develop new universalist principles in public service provision. In many ways, Covid-19 made these policies even more relevant. This means there is an alternative framework to the asset economy readily available, a set of policies that can be implemented to reform the structures that reproduce inequality within society. In simple terms, what makes it a Keynesian approach is that it seeks to reform taxation measures and provide public services along 'universalist' principles—both would substantially redress economic inequality. What makes it twenty-first-century principles rather than more traditional Keynesian measures, is the vision of the state as safeguarding equity by contributing to an ecologically sustainable and care-led well-being economy—replacing endless growth cycles of boom, bust, bailout, austerity. This signals a transformation in public policy as a coordinator of investment in green transition and social infrastructure—rather than a prognosticator of boom and bust.

Yet as indicated, this is not simply a return to what we know; what makes the new paradigm care-led and thus different from the post-war Welfare State, and this is the universal welfare aspect, is a focus on investing in social provision. For contemporary economic policymakers, this is the non-market or third-sphere, often treated as another realm of 'social' policy. The term 'care economy' refers to the overlapping provision of care by the private and public sectors but also unpaid care in the domestic sphere, or the household. The 'social infrastructures' of the national economy are health, education, culture, local communities, as key institutions that enable the social reproduction of society. Public policy is the tool used by the state to invest in both physical and social infrastructure to ensure the well-being of its citizens. Investment in care could create over two and a half times as many jobs as investment in construction (Women's Budget Group 2021a). A green and care-led recovery (New Economy Brief 2021), with a major focus on investment in disadvantaged areas would start building the critical infrastructure—both physical and social—needed for a thriving ecological sustainable economy.

6.4   Transformative Politics is Needed, not Technocratic Fixes

This is all great, applying quick and easy policy fixes to stop the widening of inequality and potentially reverse some suffering and hardship. Having said that, we are more than aware that such quick fixes are always easily reversed and at risk of falling victim to populism and economic ideologies, as history has shown repeatedly.

Our final remarks focus on the overall satisfaction that academics feel when studying to understand a topic fully with the most up-to-date information, putting forward what we truly think are necessary polity tools to prevent further harm to society from widening inequality. Theoretically, as academics, it is clear the study of inequality needs to go beyond such economistic frameworks and solutions. Inequality is multifaceted—stratifying society along the fault lines of class as well gender and race but there are other scales (like ecological) and intersections (for instance, citizenship, disability, age). To address this on a deeper level we need new concepts; we need to change our understanding of the economy, of work, of well-being, and of the meaning of equality.

We believe a care-led policy paradigm as referred to in the previous section will make life better for many and bring about greater social cohesion and economic stability. However, we also acknowledge that public policy means little in the everyday life and language of people. Addressing the cause of inequality means addressing the politics that make it possible and routinely justify it. Technical fixes can only improve the outcomes of the global capitalist system, not the system itself. Thus, for humanity to be free from inequality of existence, or at the very least if the lives of those suffering imminently and acutely are to be improved, our plea to policymakers and the public is to look more closely at what inequality does and ask if this is morally acceptable.

REFERENCES

Blundell, R., R. Joyce, M.C. Dias, and X. Xu. 2020. *Covid-19: The impacts of the pandemic on inequality* [Briefing note]. Institute for Fiscal Studies (IFS).

Earle, J., C. Moran, and Z. Ward-Perkins. 2016. The econocracy: The perils of leaving economics to the experts. *Manchester Capitalism*. Manchester: Manchester University Press.

Financial Times. 2020. Majority of UK public supports windfall taxes, 17 May.

Goldin, I. 2021. Covid19 has made fighting inequality more critical than ever. *Financial Times*, 6 September.

McCann, P., and R. Ortega-Argiles. 2021, November. The UK 'geography of discontent': Narratives, Brexit and inter-regional 'levelling up'. *Cambridge Journal of Regions, Economy and Society* 14 (3): 545–564.

Mian, A.R., L. Straub, and A. Sufi, 2021. What explains the decline in r*? Rising income inequality versus demographic shifts. SSRN Scholarly Paper, 22 September. Rochester, NY: Social Science Research Network. https://doi.org/10.2139/ssrn.3916345.

New Economy Brief. 2021. Briefing note: A green and care-led recovery. In *Briefing Notes*. Available at: https://wbg.org.uk/blog/briefing-note-a-spending-review-for-a-green-and-care-led-recovery/. Accessed 13 January 2022.

NY Times. 2020. A wealth tax is the logical way to support coronavirus relief, 21 April.

The Guardian. 2021. More than 1m children from key worker families living in poverty, says TUC, 14 July.

UK Parliament. 2021. Income Tax (charge): Volume 702, debated on Thursday 28 October 2021. Daily Hansard.

Women's Budget Group. 2021. Social Care, Gender and Covid-19. Available at: https://wbg.org.uk/wp-content/uploads/2021/03/Social-care-gender-and-Covid-19.pdf. Accessed 26 April 2021.

REFERENCES

Adkins, L. 2019. Social reproduction in the neoliberal era: Payments, leverage and the Minskian household. *Polygraph* 27: 19–33.

Adkins, L., M. Cooper, and M. Konings. 2020. *The asset economy*. Wiley.

Adkins, L., M. Cooper, and M. Konings. 2021. Class in the 21st century: Asset inflation and the new logic of inequality. *Environment and Planning A: Economy and Space* 53 (3): 548–572.

Andrew, A., S. Cattan, M.C. Dias, et al. 2020. How are mothers and fathers balancing work and family under lockdown? *Institute for Fiscal Studies.* Available at: https://www.ifs.org.uk/publications/14860.

Atkinson, A.B. 2015. *Inequality: What can be done?* Harvard University Press.

Bach, L., et al. 2020. Rich pickings? Risk, return, and skill in household wealth. *American Economic Review* 110 (9): 2703–2747.

Barker, M., and J. Russell. 2020. Feeding the food insecure in Britain: Learning from the 2020 COVID-19 crisis. *Food Security* 12: 865–870.

Bank of England. 2020a. Quantitative easing—Fact sheet, gov.co.uk, November. Available at: https://www.bankofengland.co.uk/monetary-policy/quantitative-easing. Accessed 12 November 2021.

Bank of England. 2020b. Bank of England Monetary Policy Report Press Conference, Thursday 5 November.

Bank of England. 2020c. Bank of England measures to respond to the economic shock from COVID19, 11 March.

Bank of England. 2020d. Asset Purchase Facility: Asset purchases and TFSME—Market Notice, 19 March.

Bank of England. 2020e. Remarks on COVID19 and Monetary Policy, Speech given by Professor Jonathan Haskel, External Member of the Monetary Policy Committee Brighton Chamber of Commerce, 1 July.

Bank of England. 2020f. The central bank balance sheet as a policy tool: Past, present and future, speech given by Andrew Bailey, 28 August, Jackson Hole Economic Policy Symposium.

Bank of England. 2020g. Monetary Policy Summary and minutes of the Monetary Policy Committee meeting ending on 4 August 2020.

Bank of England. 2021. Our response to coronavirus (Covid), 21 January. Available at: https://www.bankofengland.co.uk/coronavirus. Accessed 22 April 2021.

Baxter, D., R. Earwaker, and R. Casey. 2020. *Struggling renters need a lifeline.* York: Joseph Roundtree Foundation.

Beck, Roland, et al. 2019. Medium-term treatment and side-effects of quantitative easing: International evidence. ECB Working Paper No. 2229.

Benyon and Vassilev. 2021. Personal and economic wellbeing estimates by those with and without a disability, across time. Office for National Statistics.

Best, J. 2005. *The limits of transparency: Ambiguity and the history of international finance.* Ithaca, New York: Cornell University Press.

Bibby, J., G. Everest, and I. Abbs. 2020. Will Covid-19 be a watershed moment for health inequalities. *The Health Foundation.* https://www.health.org.uk/sites/default/files/2020-05/Will%20COVID-19%20be%20a%20watershed%20moment%20for%20health%20inequalities.pdf.

Blundell, R., R. Joyce, M.C. Dias, and X. Xu. 2020. *Covid-19: The impacts of the pandemic on inequality* [Briefing note]. Institute for Fiscal Studies (IFS).

BMJ. 2019. Food insecurity in UK is among worst in Europe, especially for children, says committee. *British Medical Journal* 364: 126–127.

Bonefeld, W. 1995. The Politics of Debt: Social discipline and control. *Common Sense* 17: 69–91.

Boris Johnson on Facebook 17 May 2020.

Boris Johnson, House of Commons Statement, 22 September 2020.

Boushey, H., J.B. DeLong, and M. Steinbaum. 2017. *After Piketty: The agenda for economics and inequality.* Harvard University Press.

Boyer, R. 2012. The four fallacies of contemporary austerity policies: The lost Keynesian legacy. *Cambridge Journal of Economics* 36 (1): 283–312.

Brookings. 2015. Kevin Warsh, Don Kohn on QE and inequality, 10 June.

Brown Shipley. 2020. Financial plans of the wealthy post-COVID19. Research Report. Available at https://brownshipley.com/en-gb/articles/financial-plans-of-the-wealthy-post-covid-19. Accessed 17 November 2021.

Bump, P. 2013. Obama calls inequality the "defining challenge of our time." *The Atlantic,* 4 December.

Business Insider. 2020. How business insiders saw their net worth increase by half a trillion dollars during the pandemic, 30 October.

Byrne, B., C. Alexander, and W. Shankley. 2020. *Ethnicity, race and inequality in the UK: State of the nation.* Policy Press.

Christophers, B. 2020. *Rentier capitalism: Who owns the economy, and who pays for it?* Verso Books.

CityAM. 2020. Bailey: Bank of England will reverse QE before raising rates, 22 June.

CityAM. 2021. Budget: Rishi Sunak's 'age of optimism' boosted by higher growth forecast post-Covid, 27 October.

CityWire. 2020. Labour joins chorus calling for a wealth tax, 6 July.

CNN. 2020. Coronavirus is the great equaliser, Madonna tells fans from her bathtub, 23 March.

CPAG. 2021. *Child Poverty Facts and Figures.* Child Poverty Action Group.

Credit Suisse. 2021. Credit Suisse Wealth Report 2021.

Cromarty, H. 2020. *Housing conditions in the private rented sector (England).* House of Commons Briefing Paper No. 7328, 4 February.

Crouch, C. 2009. Privatised Keynesianism: An unacknowledged policy regime. *BJPIR* 11: 382–399.

Dorling, D. 2014. *Inequality and the 1%.* London and New York: Verso Books.

Dorling, D. 2019. *Inequality and the 1%,* 2nd ed. London and New York: Verso Books.

Duncan, et al. 2021. https://www.theguardian.com/uk-news/2021/mar/30/covid-frontline-workers-priced-out-of-homeowning-in-98-of-great-britain.

Durand, M. 2015. The OECD better life initiative: How's life? And the measurement of well-being. *Review of Income and Wealth* 61 (1): 4–17.

Earle, J., C. Moran, and Z. Ward-Perkins. 2016. The econocracy: The perils of leaving economics to the experts. *Manchester Capitalism.* Manchester: Manchester University Press.

Eisenstein, Z. 2014. *Hatreds: Racialized and sexualised conflicts in the 21st century.* New York: Routledge.

Epstein, G.A. 2005. Introduction. In *Financialization and the world economy: A reader,* ed. G.A. Epstein. Cheltenham: Edward Elgar.

Evening Standard. 2020. How coronavirus is affecting the super-rich: Billionaires search for country estates and islands to avoid COVID19, 19 March.

Fagereng, A., et al. 2020. Heterogeneity and persistence in returns to wealth. *Econometrica* 88 (1): 115–170.

Financial Conduct Authority. 2020a. Joint statement by the FCA, FRC and PRA. Available at: https://www.fca.org.uk/news/statements/joint-statement-fca-frc-pra. Accessed 26 April 2021.

Financial Conduct Authority. 2020b. Mortgages and coronavirus: Information for consumers. Available at: https://www.fca.org.uk/consumers/mortgages-coronavirus-consumers. Accessed 25 April 2021.

Financial Conduct Authority. 2021a. Financial Lives 2020 survey: The impact of coronavirus, 11 February. Available at: https://www.fca.org.uk/publication/research/financial-lives-survey-2020.pdf. Accessed 26 April 2021.

Financial Conduct Authority. 2021b. Financial Conduct Authority. 2020a. Coronavirus: information for consumers with personal loans, overdrafts and other forms of credit. Available at: https://www.fca.org.uk/consumers/coronavirus-information-personal-loans-credit-cards-overdrafts. Accessed 30 April 2021.

Financial Reporter. 2022. Pensions remain a bigger share of wealth than property, 7 January.

Financial Times. 2015. Four reasons why QE will be different in the eurozone, 20 January.

Financial Times. 2020a. Pension funds suffer record losses as COVID19 hits, 30 April.

Financial Times. 2020b. Mark Carney warns coronavirus will hit the UK economy, 28 February.

Financial Times. 2020c. How does QE help the coronavirus problem?, 27 March.

Financial Times. 2020d. BOE makes emergency rate cut to cushion economy, 11 March.

Financial Times. 2020e. Coronavirus fallout Bank of England launches 4 key measures, 11 March.

Financial Times. 2020f. Bank of England boosts bond-buying by £100bn but slows the pace, 18 June.

Financial Times. 2020g. Don't fight the Fed but don't depend on it either, 6 July.

Financial Times. 2020h. Andrew Bailey says BoE has ample 'firepower' to support UK economy, 28 August.

Financial Times. 2020i. Coronavirus fallout Bank of England launches 4 key measures, 11 March.

Financial Times. 2020j. UK to stop using RPI inflation measure in 2030, 25 November.

Financial Times. 2020k. Majority of UK public supports windfall taxes, 17 May.

Financial Times. 2021a. COVID19: Widening the gap between rich and poor, 16 February.

Financial Times. 2021b. Budget will leave millions worse off next year, studies find, 28 October.

Financial Times. 2022. Investment and the multiple risks of 2022, 6 January.

Financial Times Adviser. 2020a. Pension see COVID recovery but annuities stay low, 4 August.

Financial Times Adviser. 2021a. CGT gets another reprieve on 'tax day', 23 March.

Finland Ministry of Social Affairs. 2019. Preliminary Results of the Basic Income Experiment: Self-perceived wellbeing improved, during the first year no effects on employment. https://stm.fi/en/-/perustulokokeilun-alustavat-tul okset-hyvinvointi-koettiin-paremmaksi-ensimmaisena-vuonna-ei-tyollisyysva ikutuksia.

Food and Agricultural Organisation (FAO). 2018. *The state of food security and nutrition in the world: Building climate resilience for food security and nutrition*. FAO: Rome.

Forbes. 2015. How Federal Reserve Quantitative Easing Expanded Wealth Inequality, 25 June.

Francis-Devine, B. 2021. Coronavirus: Impact on household debt and savings. House of Commons Library. Available at: https://researchbriefings.files.parlia ment.uk/documents/CBP-9060/CBP-9060.pdf. Accessed 28 April 2021.

Froud, J., C. Haslam, S. Johal, and K. Williams. 2000. Restructuring for share-holder value and its implications for labour. *Cambridge Journal of Economics* 24 (6): 771–797.

Froud, J., S. Johal, C. Haslam, and K. Williams. 2001. Accumulation under conditions of inequality. *Review of International Political Economy* 8 (1): 66–95.

FT. 2022. Prospering in the pandemic: The winners and losers of the Covid era, 3 January.

Gabor, D. 2020. Why you shouldn't fall for the panic about Britain's public debt. *The Guardian*. https://www.theguardian.com/commentisfree/2020/oct/29/panic-britain-public-debt-government-borrowing-pandemic.

Gamble, A. 2014. *Crisis without end?: The unravelling of Western prosperity*. Palgrave Macmillan.

Giles, C. 2016. UK suffering 'first lost decade since 1860s' says Carney. *Financial Times*, 5 December. Available at: https://www.ft.com/content/c0c36268-bb0d-11e6-8b45-b8b81dd5d080. Aaccessed 16 March 2022.

GMO. 2021. Waiting for the last dance: The hazards of asset allocation in at a late stage major bubble. Available at: https://www.gmo.com/europe/res earch-library/waiting-for-the-last-dance/. Accessed 11 January 2022.

Goldin, I. 2021. Covid19 has made fighting inequality more critical than ever. *Financial Times*, 6 September.

Hancock, Matt. 2020. BBC daily coronavirus address, 19 April.

Hancock, Matt. 2021. BBC Breakfast, 13 January.

Haque, Z., L. Becares, and N. Treloar. 2021. *Over-exposed and under-protected* (p. 24) [Research Report]. Runnymede Trust.

Harari, D., M. Keep, and P. Brien. 2021. *Coronavirus: Economic Impact*. London: House of Commons. Available at: https://researchbriefings.files. parliament.uk/documents/CBP-8866/CBP-8866.pdf. Accessed 13 January 2021.

Hardie, I. 2021. The impact of universal credit rollout on housing security: An analysis of landlord repossession rates in English local authorities. *Journal of Social Policy* 50 (2): 225–246. https://doi.org/10.1017/S00472794200 00021.

Harvey, D. 2014. Afterthoughts on Piketty's Capital. http://davidharvey.org/ 2014/05.

Hay, C. 2009. Good inflation, bad inflation: The housing boom, economic growth and the disaggregation of inflationary preferences in the UK and Ireland. *The British Journal of Politics & International Relations* 11 (3): 461–478.

Hay, C. 2011. Pathology without crisis? The strange demise of the Anglo-Liberal growth model. *Government and Opposition* 46 (1): 1–31.

Hay, C. 2013. *The failure of Anglo-Liberal capitalism*. Palgrave Macmillan.

Hedrick-Wong, Y. 2015. QE And Its Global Consequences. *Forbes*, 18 October.

Henau, J. D., and S. Himmelweit. 2020. *A Care-led Recovery from Coronavirus*. Women's Budget Group.

HM Treasury. 2020. Eat Out to Help Out launches today - with government paying half on restaurant bills, 3 August. Available at: https://www.gov.uk/ government/news/eat-out-to-help-out-launches-today-with-government-pay ing-half-on-restaurant-bills. Accessed 19 May 2021.

HM Treasury. 2021. Budget Speech 2021. Available at: https://www.gov.uk/ government/speeches/budget-speech-2021. Accessed 15 April 2021.

HM Treasury and Sunak MP, T.R.H.R. 2020a. A Plan for Jobs speech, 8 July. Available at: https://www.gov.uk/government/speeches/a-plan-for-jobs-speech. Accessed 2 May 2021.

HMRC. 2020. HMRC coronavirus (COVID-19) statistics, gov.co.uk, 12 May. Available at: https://www.gov.uk/government/collections/hmrc-cor onavirus-covid-19-statistics. Accessed 12 November 2021.

Hohberger, S., R. Priftis, and L. Vogel. 2019. The macroeconomic effects of quantitative easing in the euro area: Evidence from an estimated DSGE model. *Journal of Economic Dynamics and Control* 108: 103756. https:// doi.org/10.1016/j.jedc.2019.103756.

Hohberger, et al. 2019. The distributional effect of conventional monetary policy and quantitative easing: Evidence from an estimated DSGE model. Bank of Canada Staff Working Paper 2019-6.

Homeless Monitor. 2021. Crisis. https://www.crisis.org.uk/ending-homelessn ess/homelessness-knowledge-hub/homelessness-monitor/england/the-hom elessness-monitor-england-2021/.

Homelessness Monitor. 2017. Crisis. https://www.crisis.org.uk/ending-hom elessness/homelessness-knowledge-hub/homelessness-monitor/england/the-homelessness-monitor-england-2017/.

Honohan, P. 2019. Should Monetary Policy Take Inequality and Climate Change into Account?

Hope, D., and J. Limberg. 2022. The economic consequences of major tax cuts for the rich. Socio-Economic Review, mwab061. https://doi.org/10.1093/ser/mwab061.

House of Commons. 2021a. *Coronavirus: Universal Credit during the Crisis.* House of Commons Briefing Paper No. 8999, 15 January.

House of Commons. 2021b. *Coronavirus: Impact on household savings and debt.* House of Commons Briefing Paper No. 9060.

Houses of Parliament. 2021. https://commonslibrary.parliament.uk/research-bri efings/cbp-9060/.

Human Rights Watch (HRW). 2019. https://www.hrw.org/report/2019/05/20/nothing-left-cupboards/austerity-welfare-cuts-and-right-food-uk.

Hutton, G. 2020. Eat Out to Help Out Scheme. House of Commons Library. Available at: https://commonslibrary.parliament.uk/research-briefings/cbp-8978/. Accessed 19 May 2021.

Hutton, G., and N. Foley. 2021. *Hospitality Industry and Covid-19, CBP 91.* London: House of Commons Library. Available at: https://commonslibrary.parliament.uk/research-briefings/cbp-9111/. Accessed 19 May 2021.

IFS. 2017. In work poverty among families with children. Available at: https://ifs.org.uk/uploads/publications/comms/r129_ch5.pdf. Accessed 14 December 2021.

IFS. 2020. Trends in Economic Inequality. The IFS Deaton Review.

IFS. 2021. Inequalities in education, skills and incomes in the UK: The implications of the COVID19 pandemic, March.

Inside Housing. 2020. The housing pandemic: Four graphs showing the link between COVID-19 deaths and the housing crisis. https://www.insidehou sing.co.uk/insight/insight/the-housing-pandemic-four-graphs-showing-the-link-between-covid-19-deaths-and-the-housing-crisis-66562.

Ipsos MORI. 2020. Majority of public support making £20 per week Universal Credit uplift permanent, 18 December.

Joseph Roundtree Foundation. 2020. Coalition warns it would be a terrible mistake to cut the £20 uplift to Universal Credit, 29 November.

Joseph Roundtree Foundation. 2021a. The Living Standards Outlook 2021, January.

Joseph Roundtree Foundation. 2021b. *UK Poverty 2020–21, the leading independent report.* London: Joseph Roundtree Foundation.

Jung, J., J. Manley, and V. Shrestha. 2021. Coronavirus infections and deaths by poverty status: The effects of social distancing. *Journal of Economic Behavior & Organization* 182: 311–330.

Kabeer, N., S. Razavi, and Y. van der Meulen Rodgers. 2021. Feminist economic perspectives on the COVID-19 pandemic. *Feminist Economics* 27 (1–2): 1–29. https://doi.org/10.1080/13545701.2021.1876906.

Khan, O. 2020. *The Colour of Money: Race and economic inequality*. Runneymead Trust. Available at: https://www.runnymedetrust.org/blog/the-colour-of-money-race-and-economic-inequality. Accessed 31 January 2022.

Knight Frank. 2021. The Wealth Report. Available at: https://www.knightfrank.com/wealthreport. Accessed 20 January 2022.

Kollewe, J. 2021. UK house prices rise at fastest rate since 2004 amid stamp duty rush, 29 June.

Krippner, G.R. 2011. *Capitalizing on crisis: The political origins of the rise of finance*. Cambridge, MA: Harvard University Press.

Kuznets, S. 1955. Economic growth and income inequality. *The American Economic Review, American Economic Association* 45 (1): 1–28.

Lamie-Mumford, H., and A. Green. 2017. Austerity, welfare reform and the rising use of food banks by children in England and Wales. *Area* 49 (3): 273–279.

Lansley, S. 2012. *The cost of inequality: Why equality is essential for recovery*. Gibson Square.

Langley, P. 2020. Assets and assetization in financialized capitalism. *Review of International Political Economy* 28 (2): 382–393.

Lazonick, W., and M. O'Sullivan. 2000. Maximizing shareholder value: A new ideology for corporate governance. *Economy and Society* 29 (1): 13–35.

Leslie, J., and K. Shah. 2021. The Wealth Gap Year: The impact of the coronavirus crisis on UK household wealth. The Resolution Foundation. Available at: https://www.resolutionfoundation.org/app/uploads/2021/07/Wealth-gap-year.pdf.

Lowe, S.G., B.A. Searle, and S.J. Smith. 2012. from housing wealth to mortgage debt: The emergence of Britain's asset-shaped welfare state. *Social Policy and Society* 11 (1): 105–116.

Macartney, H. 2019. *The bank culture debate: Ethics, values and financialisation in Anglo-America*. Oxford University Press.

Malpass, P. 2008. Housing and the New Welfare State: Wobbly pillar or cornerstone? *Housing Studies* 23 (1): 1–19.

McCann, P., and R. Ortega-Argiles. 2021, November. The UK 'geography of discontent': Narratives, Brexit and inter-regional 'levelling up'. *Cambridge Journal of Regions, Economy and Society* 14 (3): 545–564.

Mian, A.R., L. Straub, and A. Sufi, 2021. What explains the decline in r*? Rising income inequality versus demographic shifts. SSRN Scholarly Paper,

22 September. Rochester, NY: Social Science Research Network. https://doi.org/10.2139/ssrn.3916345.

Money Charity. 2021. United Kingdom Monthly Money Statistics Report. Available at: Statistics Archive | The Money Charity. Accessed 13 January 2022.

Mongiovi, G. 2015. Piketty on capitalism and inequality: A radical economics perspective. *Review of Radical Political Economics* 47 (4): 558–565.

Montgomerie, J. 2016. Austerity and the household: The politics of economic storytelling. *British Politics* 11 (4): 418–437.

Montgomerie, J., and M. Büdenbender. 2015. Round the houses: Homeownership and failures of asset-based welfare in the United Kingdom. *New Political Economy* 20 (3): 386–405. https://doi.org/10.1080/13563467.2014.951429.

Montgomerie, J., and D. Tepe-Belfrage. 2017. Caring for debts: How the household economy exposes the limits of financialisation. *Critical Sociology* 43 (4–5): 653–668.

Montgomerie, J., and D. Tepe-Belfrage. 2020. Financialisation, crisis and austerity as the distribution of harm. In *The Routledge Handbook of Critical European Studies*. Routledge.

Moore, B., and C. Evans. 2020. Tackling Childhood Food Poverty in the UK. Leed Policy Briefs. https://eprints.whiterose.ac.uk/168869/1/PolicyLeeds-Brief4_Childhood-Food-Poverty.pdf.

MSCI. 2022. MSCI World Index. Available at: https://www.msci.com/documents/10199/149ed7bc-316e-4b4c-8ea4-43fcb5bd6523. Accessed 11 January 2022.

Mulvale, J., and D. Delaney. 2006. *Advancing economic security for women through basic income: Soundings in Saskatchewan*. Regina: Provincial Association of Transition Houses and Services of Saskatchewan.

Nazroo, J.Y. 2003. The structuring of ethnic inequalities in health: Economic position, racial discrimination, and racism. *American Journal of Public Health* 93 (2): 277–284. American Public Health Association. https://doi.org/10.2105/AJPH.93.2.277.

National Education Union (NEU). 2021. Child Poverty. https://neu.org.uk/press-releases/child-poverty.

NBER. 2020. Fifty Shades of QE: Comparing findings of central bankers and academics. NBER Working Papers 27849.

New Economy Brief. 2021. Briefing note: A green and care-led recovery. In *Briefing Notes*. Available at: https://wbg.org.uk/blog/briefing-note-a-spending-review-for-a-green-and-care-led-recovery/. Accessed 13 January 2022.

NHS Scotland. 2018. 4. Child Poverty in Scotland: Health impact and health inequalities. NHS. http://www.healthscotland.scot/media/2186/child-poverty-impact-inequalities-2018.pdf.

Nokes, C. 2021. The gendered economic impact of Covid-19. *BBC Radio 4 - Woman's Hour*. London. Available at: https://www.bbc.co.uk/programmes/m000s186. Accessed 16 March 2022.

Nunn, A. 2015. Unpicking Piketty's Problems: The Production and Reproduction of Inequality in Times of Austerity, Paper to ESRC Workshop, London, December.

Nunn, A., and D. Tepe-Belfrage. Forthcoming. Disciplinary neo-liberalisation and the new politics of inequality. *British Journal of Criminology*.

NY Times. 2020. A wealth tax is the logical way to support coronavirus relief, 21 April.

OBR. 2020. Coronavirus analysis. Available at: https://obr.uk/coronavirus-analysis/. Accessed 20 January 2022.

OBR. 2021. October 2021 economic outlook. Available at: https://obr.uk/download/economic-and-fiscal-outlook-october-2021/. Accessed 11 January 2022.

O'Connell, R., J. Brannen, and A. Knight. 2018. https://blogs.bmj.com/bmj/2018/08/15/holiday-hunger-requires-radical-long-term-solutions/.

O'Hara, S. 2014. Everything needs care: Towards a context-based economy. In *Counting on Marilyn Waring: New Advances in Feminist Economics*, ed. M. Bjørnholt and A. McKay. Demeter Press.

ONS. 2018. Total Wealth in Great Britain: April 2016 to March 2018. Available at: https://www.ons.gov.uk/peoplepopulationandcommunity/personalandhouseholdfinances/incomeandwealth/bulletins/totalwealthingreatbritain/april2016tomarch2018. Accessed 17 November 2021.

ONS. 2020. Personal and economic well-being in Great Britain. Office for National Statistics. Available at: https://www.ons.gov.uk/peoplepopulationandcommunity/wellbeing/bulletins/personalandeconomicwellbeingintheuk/january2021#savings-borrowing-and-affordability. Accessed 12 November 2021.

ONS. 2021. Personal and economic well-being in Great Britain: January 2021. Available at: https://www.ons.gov.uk/peoplepopulationandcommunity/wellbeing/bulletins/personalandeconomicwellbeingintheuk/january2021#savings-borrowing-and-affordability. Accessed 14 December 2021.

Parker, G., D. Strauss, and T. Stubbington. 2021. Budget 2021: Rishi Sunak sets out 'moral' mission to limit state and cut taxes. *Financial Times*, 27 October. Available at: https://www.ft.com/content/e7c84fbe-0857-4de8-85c1-ed81f870a4f5. Accessed 12 November 2021.

Pickett, K. 2019. What's the best way to tackle health inequalities? In *Rethinking Britain: Policy Ideas for the Many*, ed. S. Konzelmann, S. Himmelweit, J. Smith, and J. Weeks, 198–201. London: Policy Press.

Pickett, K., and R. Wilkinson. 2010. *The Spirit Level: Why Equality Is Better for Everyone*. Penguin UK.

Piketty, T. 2014. *Capital in the Twenty-First Century*, trans. A. Goldhammer. Cambridge, MA: Harvard University Press.

Powell, A., and B. Francis-Devine. 2022. Coronavirus: Impact on the labour market. Available at: https://commonslibrary.parliament.uk/research-briefings/cbp-8898/. Accessed 16 March 2022.

Public Health England. 2020. Disparities in the risk and outcomes of COVID-19. *Association of Medical Research Charities*. https://assets.publishing.service.gov.uk/government/uploads/system/uploads/attachment_data/file/908434/Disparities_in_the_risk_and_outcomes_of_COVID_August_2020_update.pdf.

Rajan, R. 2010. *Fault lines: How hidden fractures still threaten the world economy*, Vol. New ed. Princeton, NJ: Princeton University Press, Woodstock.

Resolution Foundation. 2020. Who Gains? The importance of accounting for capital gains, Resolution Foundation, May.

Resolution Foundation. 2021a. (Wealth) Gap Year: The impact of the coronavirus crisis on UK household wealth, July.

Resolution Foundation. 2021b. After Shocks: Financial resilience before and during the COVID19 crisis, April.

Reuters. 2020a. Central banks' eye on inequality makes QE uncomfortable, 2 October.

Reuters. 2020b. Cresting "first wave" of stimulus may be next hurdle for world markets, 16 July.

Reuters. 2020c. UK delays change to RPI inflation in boost for bond buying investments, 25 November.

Reuters. 2021. In 2020 the ultra-rich got richer. Now they are bracing for the backlash, 25 March.

Reuters. 2022. Fed signals trigger world stocks, bonds sell off, 6 January.

Rishi Sunak MP. 2021. Budget Speech 2021. Autumn Statementpresented at the Budget, House of Commons, UK Parliament, 27 October. Available at: https://www.gov.uk/government/speeches/budget-speech-2021. Accessed 12 November 2021.

Ronald, L., et al. 2017. Whatever happened to asset-based welfare? *Shifting Approaches to Housing Wealth and Welfare Security, Policy and Politics* 45 (2): 173–193.

Ronald, R. 2008. *The ideology of home ownership: Homeowner societies and the role of housing*. New York: Palgrave Macmillan, Basingstoke.

Ronald, R., and M. Elsinga, eds. 2012. *Beyond home ownership: Housing, welfare and society*. London: Routledge.

RSA. 2020. COVID-19 vaccine deployment: Behaviour, ethics, misinformation and policy strategies. *Royal Society*, 21 October.

Savage, M. 2021. *The return of inequality: Social change and the weight of the past*. Harvard University Press.

Savills. 2021. UK housing value hits record £7.56 trillion high, 12 March.

Schwartz, H., and L. Seabrooke. 2008. Varieties of residential capitalism in the international political economy: Old welfare states and the new politics of housing. *Comparative European Politics* 6 (2): 237–261.

Shelter. 2019. This is England: A picture of Homelessness in 2019. https://england.shelter.org.uk/professional_resources/policy_and_research/policy_library/this_is_england_a_picture_of_homelessness_in_2019.

Shelter. 2021. Denied the right to a safe home: Factsheet. https://england.shelter.org.uk/professional_resources/policy_and_research/policy_library/denied_the_right_to_a_safe_home_factsheet.

Sky. 2021. Cut to universal credit uplift 'not the right way to save government money' says Gordon Brown, 4 October.

Social Attitudes Survey. 2019. British Social Attitudes Survey 37, NatCen. Available at: https://natcen.ac.uk/our-research/research/british-social-attitudes/. Accessed 17 November 2021.

Social Metrics Commission. 2020. Measuring Poverty 2020. https://socialmetricscommission.org.uk/measuring-poverty-2020/.

Solow, R.M. 1974. Intergenerational equity and exhaustible resources. *The Review of Economic Studies* [Oxford University Press, Review of Economic Studies, Ltd.] 41: 29–45.

Sparkes, M., and J.D.G. Wood. 2021. The political economy of household debt & The Keynesian policy paradigm. *New Political Economy* 26 (4): 598–615. Routledge. https://doi.org/10.1080/13563467.2020.1782364.

StepChange. 2021. Preventing a COVID arrears crisis: Financial support package for renters, 27 May.

Stiglitz, J.E., A. Sen, and J.-P. Fitoussi. 2010. *Mismeasuring our lives: Why GDP doesn't add up.* New York: The New Press.

Streeck, W. 2014. *Buying time: The delayed crisis of democratic capitalism.* Verso Books.

Syll, L. 2014. Piketty and the limits of marginal productivity theory. *Real World Economics Review* 69: 36–43.

Tax Justice UK. 2022. New figures show wealth and equality was entrenched before Covid, 7 January.

Team, V., and L. Manderson. 2020. How COVID-19 Reveals Structures of Vulnerability. *Medical Anthropology* 39 (8): 671–674. https://doi.org/10.1080/01459740.2020.1830281

The Big Issue. 2021. Thousands became homeless during pandemic with more feared in Autumn, 9 September.

The Economist. 2020. House prices in the rich world are booming, 8 April.

The Economist. 2021. Boris Johnson's Conservatives plan to create a bigger, busier state, 11 March. Available at: https://www.economist.com/britain/

2021/11/06/boris-johnsons-conservatives-plan-to-create-a-bigger-busier-state. Accessed 12 November 2021.

The Guardian. 2019. Britain risks heading to US levels of inequality, warns top economist, 14 May.

The Guardian. 2020a. The only V shaped recovery after coronavirus will be in the stock markets, 18 August.

The Guardian. 2020b. Coronavirus: British pension set to take a hit from market tumbled, 29 February.

The Guardian. 2020c. From now, policies must put young people first. Starting with the triple lock pension, 19 June.

The Guardian. 2020d. Under cover of capital gains, the hyper rich have been getting richer than we thought, 21 May.

The Guardian. 2020e. The Guardian view on COVID-19 economics: the austerity con of deficit hysteria, 14 July.

The Guardian. 2020f. For the Covid economic recovery look to the Treasury, not the bank, 1 November.

The Guardian. 2021a. Number of billionaires in UK reached new record during Covid crisis, 21 May.

The Guardian. 2021b. Renter activists block London eviction as end of COVID protections takes toll, 24 November.

The Guardian. 2021c. Rise in women sleeping rough is hidden in England, charities warn, 30 June.

The Guardian. 2021d. Ministers have no clear plan to tackle child poverty, say cross-party MPs, 22 September.

The Guardian. 2021e. Treasury could raise £16 billion a year if shares and property were taxed like salaries, 26 October.

The Guardian. 2021f. More than 1m children from key worker families living in poverty, says TUC, 14 July.

The Health Foundation. 2021. *Unequal Pandemic, fairer recovery: The covid-19 impact inquiry report, July 2021*. London: The Health Foundation.

The Independent. 2020. Disabled people denied benefit uplift during pandemic because it would be "too complicated" for DWP IT system, 18 November.

The Independent. 2021a. UK billionaires see fortunes saw in pandemic, 21 May.

The Independent. 2021b. People living in poverty 'hit harder by gas and electricity bills', new data shows, 24 October.

The Independent. 2022. Wealth of the richest one percent in UK more than 230 times that of the poorest 10%, ONS says, 9 January.

The Metro. 2021a. Almost 100,000 families were homeless at the beginning of 2021, 22 April.

The Metro. 2021b. Malnutrition doubles to over 10,000 cases under Tory rule, 8 November.

The Metro. 2021c. Marcus Rashford forces another government U-Turn on free school meals, 8 November.

The Mirror. 2021. Foodbanks hand out 32 meals every minute—And it's about to get worse, 24 November.

Toussaint, J., and M. Elsinga. 2009. Exploring 'housing asset-based welfare': Can the UK be held up as an example for Europe? *Housing Studies* 24 (5): 669–692.

Tower Halmets. 2018. Healthy life expectancy in Tower Hamlets: Annual public health report of the director of public health. Tower Hamlets.

Trades Union Congress. 2020/2021. TUC poll: 7 in 10 requests for furlough turned down for working mums. News Listing, Organisation, 14 January. Available at: https://www.tuc.org.uk/news/tuc-poll-7-10-requests-furlough-turned-down-working-mums. Accessed 28 April 2121.

Trussell Trust. 2021. More than 5,100 food parcels given to people facing crisis across the UK every day in past six months, says the Trussell Trust, 24 November.

Trust for London. 2021. Homelessness and rough sleeping in the time of COVID19. Available at: https://www.trustforlondon.org.uk/publications/homelessness-and-rough-sleeping-in-the-time-of-covid-19/. Accessed 15 December 2021.

UBS. 2020. Riding the storm, Billionaires insights 2020. Available at: https://www.ubs.com/content/dam/static/noindex/wealth-management/ubs-billionaires-report-2020-spread.pdf. Accessed 19 November 2021.

UK Parliament. 2020. Income Inequality in the UK: Research briefing, 13 August.

UK Parliament. 2021. Income Tax (charge): Volume 702, debated on Thursday 28 October 2021. Daily Hansard.

University of Sheffield. 2018. https://www.sheffield.ac.uk/social-sciences/news/12-million-living-uk-food-deserts-studys-shows

University of Warwick. 2020. How much tax to the rich really pay you? New evidence from tax micro data in the UK. CAGE Policy Briefing Number 27, June.

Valadez, L., and D. Hirsch. 2018. *Child Poverty map of the UK January 2018*. London: End Child Poverty Coalition.

Wales Online. 2020. Almost two million children went hungry in the UK in 2020, 9 December.

Warren, T. 2006. Moving beyond the gender wealth gap: On gender, class, ethnicity, and wealth inequalities in the United Kingdom. *Feminist Economics* 12 (1–2): 195–219.

Washington Post. 2020a. Gov. Cuomo is wrong, covid-19 is anything but a great equalizer, 5th April.

Washington Post. 2020b. The pandemic is dramatically deepening inequality, 15 October.

Watson, M. 2009. Headlong into the Polanyian Dilemma: The impact of middle-class moral panic on the British Government's response to the sub-prime crisis. *British Journal of Politics and International Relations* 11 (3): 422–437.

Waylen, G. 2017. Gendering institutional change. In *The Oxford handbook of gender and politics*, ed. K. Celis, J. Kantola, S.L. Weldon, and G. Wyalen. First issued as an Oxford University Press paperback. Oxford: Oxford University Press. Available at: https://doi.org/10.1093/acrefore/9780190228637.013.237.

Wealth Tax Commission. 2020. Final report of the wealth tax commission, 9 December 2020. Wealth Tax Commission.

Whittaker, J. 2020. Modern Monetary Theory: The rise of economists who say huge government debt is not a problem. *The Conversation*, 7 July.

Williamson, S.D. 2017. Quantitative Easing: How Well Does This Tool Work? Federal Reserve Bank of St Louis, Regional Economist Q3.

Women's Budget Group. 2020. Submission to the Women and Equalities Select Committee inquiry: Unequal impact? Coronavirus and the gendered economic impact, June. Available at: https://wbg.org.uk/wp-content/uploads/2020/06/WBG-Gender-economic-impact-submission.pdf. Accessed 9 April 2021.

Women's Budget Group. 2021. Social Care, Gender and Covid-19. Available at: https://wbg.org.uk/wp-content/uploads/2021/03/Social-care-gender-and-Covid-19.pdf. Accessed 26 April 2021.

Women's Budget Group, Close the Gap, Engender, Fawcett Society, Northern Ireland Women's Budget Group and Women's Equality Network Wales. 2021. One year on: Women are less likely than men to feel the Government's response to Covid-19 has met their needs, March. Available at: https://wbg.org.uk/analysis/reports/one-year-on-women-are-less-likely-than-men-to-feel-the-governments-response-to-covid-19-has-met-their-needs/. Accessed 12 April 2021.

Wren-Lewis, S. 2014. Fiscal policy remains in the stone age. VoxEU, CEPR, 10 May 2018.

WSJ. 2020. Derby's Take: New research says central bank view on bond buying too rosey, 29 September.

Index

9 783030 969134